D1383737

Praise for *Buy Now*

"We came to Cesari Direct with a lackluster infomercial and they turned it into one of the top 10, longest-running DRTV shows of its time. Whether it's creating, filming, or marketing new ideas, Cesari Direct is who you want on your DRTV project."

—Allan Gourlie
Owner, Quick N Brite

"Rick Cesari is someone who [has] changed my life forever. He had the vision and fortitude to help us pursue our dreams of teaching and reaching millions of people, which seemingly happened overnight. I recommend Rick to anyone looking to manifest their dreams through direct sales."

—Jay Kordich
Father of Juicing and *New York Times* best-selling
Author of *The Juiceman's Power of Juicing*

"1414 Dexter Avenue in Seattle, WA, is the home of a true, direct-response pioneer. Rick Cesari was the architect behind one of the biggest brands to emerge out of the infomercial world: The George Foreman Grill. Rick and DRTV Cesari Direct set the gold standard and demonstrated to the world that, when harnessed correctly, there are no limits to the reach and power of direct response."

—Anthony Sullivan
Star of Discovery TV's *Pitchman* and DRTV Producer

BUY NOW

BUY NOW

CREATIVE MARKETING THAT GETS CUSTOMERS TO RESPOND TO YOU AND YOUR PRODUCT

RICK CESARI
RON LYNCH
WITH **TOM KELLY**

WILEY

John Wiley & Sons, Inc.

Published by John Wiley & Sons, Inc., Hoboken, New Jersey.
Published simultaneously in Canada.

For general information on our other products and services or for technical support, please contact our Customer Care Department within the United States at (800) 762-2974, outside the United States at (317) 572-3993 or fax (317) 572-4002.

Wiley also publishes its books in a variety of electronic formats. Some content that appears in print may not be available in electronic books. For more information about Wiley products, visit our web site at www.wiley.com.

Library of Congress Cataloging-in-Publication Data:
Cesari, Rick, 1956-
  Buy now : creative marketing that gets customers to respond to you and your product / Rick Cesari, Ron Lynch ; with Tom Kelly.
      p. cm.
  ISBN 978-0-470-88801-8 (hardback)
  ISBN 978-1-118-00787-7 (ebk)
  ISBN 978-1-118-00788-4 (ebk)
  ISBN 978-1-118-00789-1 (ebk)
1. Direct marketing. 2. Customer relations. I. Lynch, Ron, 1966- II. Kelly, Tom, 1950 Oct. 8- III. Title.
  HF5415.126.C44 2011
  658.8'72--dc22
                                                                           2010037971

Printed in the United States of America

10 9 8 7 6 5 4 3 2 1

CONTENTS

PROLOGUE

The Secret to Our Success

Entrepreneurs, Fortune 500 companies and small companies thinking big come to us every day and say, "Hey, what you did for OxiClean: I want that!" "What you did for the Juiceman Juicer, for the George Foreman Grill, for the Sonicare toothbrush. . . . We want a brand. We want *that!*"

The next thing they usually say is, "But I don't want a yell-and-sell pitchman like Billy Mays!"

It's funny that everybody who walks through our door makes some pretty universal assumptions about what goes on here. We don't—assume, that is. That's our first rule. Don't assume. Don't assume you know everything about anything. That's the first sign of arrogance and the last sign of learning. Want to stop creativity? Tell people you know everything, and act like it's the absolute fact. Our job is to walk into every situation with innocence, newness, and freshness, and that starts with ignorance. The same ignorance your next unassuming customer has when he or she finds you in the marketplace for the first time.

Together we have sold somewhere north of $2 billion worth of product and launched about 30 brands. We are proven to be some of the world's best salesmen, but it is not because of what we say. It is because we know what to *listen to*.

Ever had a really good doctor? A really good coach? Or meet a really good salesperson? I bet they all had the same common thread. They ask questions—lots of questions. They listen. They observe. They observe even more. They ask other people what their experience has been around you. They align their observations and their learning with years of proven experience. They strategize. They plan. They communicate. They get your commitment and buy in to the result that will benefit *you* the most.

Then, the very last thing they do is . . . start.

That is what we do every day. It is the secret to our success.

Yes, we have had unparalleled success and good fortune. Often we have been in the right place at the right time. We have also had failures you've never heard about. We'll share some here. Yet the truth is, we wouldn't be a leader in the direct response (DR) marketing space based on just a good 25-year run of pure luck. Our expertise is not machismo, or a flag we plant for attention. It is, rather, time-tested, results-oriented, and statistically proven. Our kind of success is one that transfers from boardroom dialogue to actual spreadsheet success, real product sales, increased brand equity, and return on shareholder dividends. Like everything we seek to do, we keep a scorecard and count our success—not with gold trophies, New York gala dinners, or personality features in *Adweek*, but with units sold, customers satisfied, and dollars in the bank—for us and our clients. We're not involved in advertising art. We are in the modern digital, multichannel, marketing business. We sell. We sell more for our clients around the clock, around the world.

While you we're sleeping last night, we were busy selling.

Some of the greatest American companies today have walked through our doors. Our identity and reputation is based on a relatively simple set of principles and understandings that drive sales. In any company, sales is the healer of everything that ails you.

In the following pages, we will share the insights and knowledge we have developed over the years. This is not a book of relative philosophies on how to sell, how to manipulate the consumer, or how to get inside the head of the American housewife to sell another food processor. This is a book specifically on how we have charted a course to successfully create transactions through television, and how the radical shift of media channel explosion and the Internet threw that model on its ear. It's also a down-and-dirty exposé of how we nearly lost it all and came back with new learning and an innovative arsenal of direct marketing techniques that not only has put us back on the map, but realistically pushed us many years ahead of both traditional DR marketers and conventional advertising agencies. We've been successfully working this new model for our clients for the past five years. We have proven it works by growing revenues for our clients and expanding specific markets and individual demographic verticals. Competitive media companies routinely bring their clients to us with confidence. How many companies in the world have had their competitors come—and pay a premium—to add *your* secret sauce to their recipe? It happens in our world all of the time. Why in the world would we let them? We learned the hard way the first three rules of partnerships:

1. Never count the other guy's money.
2. Don't set out to make a million dollars from anybody.
3. Definitely set out to make one dollar from everybody.

If that sounds like hyperbole, read this book. You'll understand every bit of it before you're done.

We have perfected the secret and science of deconstructing a product and rebuilding its identity to match a new innovative category.

We create a *unique selling proposition*, a USP, for any given product. Then we pave a multifaceted, multidimensional sales path that looks slightly different to each consumer segment that approaches the product in a variety of media channels. You cannot be all things to all people, yet we systematically show our clients how to be more than one necessity to many different customers, while maintaining a broad, cohesive brand message. The beauty is, we do it in the real world, building sales and funding advertising organically the whole way.

In the following pages, we'll tell you how we use something called *Direct Demographic Media Messaging* to build brands with a Self-Funding Direct Response Campaign that crosses diverse media channels.

We'll explain how any company—your company—can use these techniques to launch a product with a high probability of success.

We'll explain why direct response sales never cannibalize retail store sales. In fact, they enhance them.

We'll even tell you how we have employed strategies to make small companies look huge, huge companies look homespun, and corporate giants appear fleet-footed, friendly, and caring.

At the end of the day, just reading this book will make you a better marketer, a better businessperson, and a more valuable asset to your company, whether you have lunch in the boardroom or the break room.

Are you an entrepreneur who wants to launch your own product? This book is your personal manual, which we have created to help you grow and succeed. Please acknowledge us as having inspired you when you write your memoirs!

Are you a CEO or CMO who needs a peek under the hood of direct response to appear more knowledgeable in your next meeting, presentation, or selection of an agency? We are the CliffNotes for the course they don't teach at Harvard. You need this book. Buy one for everybody on your team. You need people who are willing to think like leaders. They know less than you; they need it!

CHAPTER
1

Why "Buy Now"?

When choosing a name for this book it was important for us to grab your attention and communicate to you two things: One, you have a strong need for something. Two, we can fulfill it. That's a hard thing to do in the brevity of a book cover, yet you did pick up the book with some degree of interest. We would like to think that we stacked the deck a little in our favor to get you to take that action. We did, in fact. In the context of this book, we'll tell you how and why; better, we'll teach you how to do it.

Understand that we are interested in your success. Most folks want to hold something that is uniquely theirs alone, a secret. We don't have a secret. The fact is, there is not one; there are many. What this book will give you is the ingredients; the secret ingredients, if you will. Every single person who has used these secrets has gained some measure of success. The key is not in the ingredients as much as in the cook. Certainly, the ingredients count; you, in fact, cannot make a success in this business without them. When you personally apply them, you bring the largest unknown quantity to the mix: the genius that is you.

This much we can tell you for sure. Direct marketing is a humbling experience. We highly recommend you bring a fair share of humility to it, or the business will provide it for you. The encouraging news is that all you need is just one hit. One at bat where you connect, and you can have the opportunity to be financially set for life—if you stay smart and keep your head in the game.

Now, why *Buy Now* as the title? First, it's a command. Not a suggestion, not an insinuation, but a real command that grabs you by the collar and tells you what to do. Does it make you buy? No. Did it make you pay attention? Absolutely! Did we choose an image of a hand with a credit card to give you the notion that there was something in it for you financially? Certainly. Why did we choose a gold card? Why the bold, open-block red font? Were these all just happenstance created by the book's publisher? Not a chance. That's just one aspect of what you'll learn in this book: how to think at a level of marketing detail that will enable you to weave such a complex web that, in the end, looks beautiful and works so simply. Like in the fairy tale "Hansel and Gretel," our goal as marketers is to lay the bread-crumbs that lead you and your customer home.

Remember, the average American is blasted by tens of thou-sands of marketing messages a day. How do you grab their atten-tion, engage them with interest, and begin a meaningful sales dialogue in just seconds? It's possible. We do it all the time. Frankly, you probably experience it all the time and don't real-ize it; you just become interested. You are drawn in.

The Direct Response Solution

We are routinely approached these days by large American corporations that are looking for our expertise and guidance to help them clear one of two primary hurdles. They want to either launch a new brand or revive a quality product that has dying sales caused by lack of attention or shelf crowding. Both are attainable through our methodology. Why the new inter-est in direct response? The answer is probably driven from a number of directions, but the easiest and most obvious one is the absolutely brutal environment out there for consumer dollars. The economy has tanked, and consumers have closed their wallets. Manufacturers are in a spin, not just to grow sales but to minimize shrinking sales as fast as they can. Stockholders are putting knives to the necks of CEOs, who are no doubt living in fear. The shift that you may not have noticed in the past decade is that "CEO" does not mean what it used to.

Once upon a time, the CEO was royalty, walking through the halls of his or her company like a god or Godzilla, leaving a trail of either bowing subjects or destruction behind. Today's CEO most likely is not the person who started the company, nor even the person hired by the company. More often today, the CEO is the person hired by the conglomerate consolidator or the venture fund that bought the company, in the hopes of reselling it to the next-highest bidder. That is the ill of the American corporation. The most senior plant manager, executive secretary, or marketing director usually has a greater idea of the lifeblood of a company than the well-educated Columbia grad who is now saddled with title of CEO *and* the blame for shrinking sales in a shriveling economy. If you are running a company in which you did not rise to the top organically, you shouldn't do a thing until you spend a week working in every department at the level at which you can do the work. Get trained in the business *before* you try to run the business.

Whom does the CEO traditionally turn to when sales need to increase? The chief marketing officer (CMO), who has an acute interest in saving his or her own skin. Blame the sales on the sales guy; and don't forget to cut his or her marketing budget and tell staff they are now accountable for every penny. Sounds dumb, but people do it all the time.

That's where we come in. One way or another, dozens of companies show up every year at our office wanting to talk about this mysterious form of advertising that allows you to directly measure sales against advertising spend. Understand, direct response marketing is not taught as a major at any university in the world. Most don't have a single class in it. All of the true experts in the field you can count on your two hands. The truly unusual fact is that direct response is one of the oldest and most perseverant forms of marketing in the history of the United States, and probably the world.

Carnival Beginnings

Now, you may know a man named Mel Arthur, he is the face and voice of the Internet phone connection device MagicJack. This is not Mel's first rodeo. He has been around the pitch business for years and has had great success on the shopping networks. Ron met him one afternoon while directing a show called the "FlavorWave Oven," in which Mel's company had an interest. He relayed a story on how he got started in the business as a kid. Mel, Ron Popeil, Arthur Morris, and a guy named Charles Bronson—yes, *that* Charles Bronson—used to go down to the Atlantic City Pier as kids, and one of their fathers (which one escapes me) would pick up cases of product that these 10- to 15-year-olds, would sell on the boardwalk all summer long. One day it would be flatware, the next day cigars, linens, handbags, kitchen knives, or beauty cream. You name it, these kids were direct-marketing it. Mel relayed that the joy he has always had from this business is in the connection with his customers. Dating back to those Atlantic City days, where he'd get return customers who were happy with the last product and engaged by his entertaining pitch style, and who looked forward to his next product. Mel really shared the joy of selling—giving people a good value on a product that would help them solve a real problem in their lives.

Something clicked. I recalled my college days of being a life-guard on the Florida beaches. I got so bored, and wanted to talk to the girls, so I started selling suntan lotions. It was really simple. People on the beach all had the same problem and didn't know it. They were at risk of getting sunburn, and hurt, and I was pointing out the problem, offering them a really good solution, creating a transaction that made me money and helped them at the same time. In that quick flashback, I realized that Ron, Mel Arthur, and I shared a certain DNA that all natural salespeople have, one that makes us a little different from the rest of the world. We know in our core that selling is good. Selling helps people. People are grateful to be sold something they truly want and need. Unlock this door in your mind and you will sell more, sell better, and care about the people you are selling to.

Why Direct Response?

The question of whether direct response is a valid form of marketing and launch vehicle is fair.

We've sat in hundreds of focus groups and asked thousands of consumers what they think of infomercials. They are, at best, bemused by them; at worst, they are hostile, even volatile about the style and tone that the word "infomercial" connotes. We understand; we still have successful clients to this day who resist the word "infomercial."

Ask the next question and you will find that about 90 percent of the exact same consumer group have called the number on the screen; they've even purchased. Most, more than once. Many don't even realize they have until pressed. Dig deeper and they will tell you that not only were they compelled, most felt they made an informed buying decision and were ultimately satisfied with the product. Why? They discovered through the program that they needed it.

Do you see it? All marketing is bad—unless, of course, it is for something I want and need.

What, after all, is an infomercial? It's really an entertaining seminar directed at a specific demographic segment that has a common set of problems. The seminar offers an explanation of an innovative solution and an opportunity to participate in trying that solution. In it, you learn the details of the innovation, and typically hear from the experts who created it, the outside experts who endorse it, and long-term and new users who rely on it. Infomercials come in primarily one length: the half-hour show; 28:30, to be exact, is the most prevalent. The offshoot of the half-hour is the 2-minute, 1-minute, and, now, 30-second spots. In the industry, these are referred to as "short forms."

Do you own a George Foreman Grill? Have you brightened your laundry with OxiClean? Gotten a better dental checkup with your Sonicare toothbrush? Or rented a Rug Doctor to clean your carpets? You are an infomercial customer. If you have considered yourself a potential customer for Viagra, Cialis, eHarmony, Overstock.com, GEICO, FreeCreditReport .com, TD AMERITRADE, or even ordered a pizza over the phone, you've been touched by our industry. Even if you tried only one of these products after seeing it in retail, you've participated in the most powerful marketing model ever created.

We are not pet rocks. As an industry with a reputation for cheesy products, slimy hosts, and phony testimonials, our industry has consistently bounced back with reputable products, quality brands, and truth-in-advertising. If you think infomercials are just for shoddy start-up gadgets or stand-alone companies that operate in the dark, think again. Hewlett-Packard, Nintendo, Range Rover, Johnson & Johnson, Microsoft, Kodak, and many more blue-chip organizations are turning to the direct response sales model because it is respected by the consumer and is an efficient and consistent form of detailed messaging; most importantly, it can be very profitable while building the brand.

This need to explain complex products in pragmatic ways has been utilized over and over, with great results by others, including Apple, Thermos, and Carnival Cruise Lines. We even saw Barack Obama create unique infomercials during the 2008 political season in an attempt to gain ground against opponents. Obama went as far to have his dubbed into Spanish to make sure he had reached a voter segment whose support he felt he needed to win. Apparently, it worked.

Today, our direct response economic model magic resides in the fact that we often, initially, can swim against the tide of brick-and-mortar retail sales. That is, if you stop and think how many hands, loading docks, distributors, freight companies, sales associates, and retailers most products pass through to get to your hands, you will be amazed. Now add an incremental cost to each step in the process; then you get to the retailer and the keystone (double the wholesale cost as the price to the consumer) to compensate for having sale merchandise at the end of the cycle. You can start to see how much of what you pay for in a product is not the product but the process.

We recapture the money spent on traditional supply chain retail economics and use the huge gap between manufacturer and consumer to buy airtime and bundle products with offers retailers generally can't touch. We deliver in a drop-ship fashion. It's basically a better deal for the house and a better deal for the consumer, and they both know it. In fact, there's an ever growing subculture of consumers worldwide who fuel our industry because they have learned the value over time.

This has not gone unnoticed by more and more companies in the past decade. Before we go deeper, it's important to stop and take a closer look at the myths that surround marketing and sales.

Often, the advertising world and the art world overlap. The personalities that are drawn to filmmaking, writing, fine arts, costuming, theater, makeup, producing, writing, and performance are frequently mixed in our medium. I often hear what I will call "art snobs" say things like, "I don't watch TV; I only watch PBS or *National Geographic*." I have to laugh: The last time I checked, those were on TV! We have even worked with TV producers who were passionately excited to tell us they did not own a television. This is similar to a homebuilder saying he doesn't have a hammer. I once saw a bumper sticker that read: "Theater is life. Film is art. Television is furniture." What a load of garbage!

Television is the form of communication that has universally changed the human experience faster and more powerfully than any technology before it. It is the definitive educational and social difference that has made the baby boomer genera- tion the most important segmentation of consumers for 50 years running. We witness real human events live. Invasions, rescues, police chases, and celebrity revelations connect us emotionally as we learn the dynamic subtleties of the entire planet from the comfort of our living rooms, our boats, RVs, or streaming on our phones. We cry. We laugh. We become enraged. We connect. Alone in our homes, in the dark, we connect. You name it, we watch it.

We went to a Dallas Cowboys game earlier this year and were amazed at the enormous television suspended from the ceiling. More amazing was witnessing how many people sitting in a stadium of 80,000 unconsciously devoted the majority of their attention to watching the jumbo screen, instead of the live game going on below it.

We as American consumers are professional television viewers. We are adept, and good at it. Because of TV we have all become incredible experts at the subtle detection of truth versus fiction. Before we go further, though, we want to expose some of the social fiction that surrounds the topic of advertising, sales, and marketing. Like saying "I don't watch television," here are some other basic myths we tell ourselves, and too often believe.

Liar, Liar, Pants on Fire

Myth 1: Advertising is a method of getting people to purchase things they do not want or need.

Truth: Humans want and need products and services. It is a very basic human drive, the "tool making" and "gath- ering" of our ancestors that ensure we are always on the lookout for something external to our being that will help us live better, happier lives. Filtering, assessing, and acquisition are unavoidable human instincts, which are good. Being consumers in the prehistoric sense is what prevented us from being consumed in the literal sense. But not all people need every product.

Most advertisers work diligently to make people aware of their products. Often highly stylized, oversexed, and abundant in fluff is the narrow scope of advertising that jumps to our consciousness when we hear the word "advertising," mainly because that powerful imagery works to leave an impression. The fact is, most advertising is ineffective, goes unnoticed, and is lacking in creativity. Our storage sensors instantly reject most because it's not speaking "to us."

Direct response has the constant, unique element of almost always pointing out a problem or a need, which the product aims to resolve for you personally. It's the very posing of the question or the problem that opens your mind to the question, "Are they talking to me?" The very direct nature is actually beneficial for the audience and helps us achieve success in particular avenues of media. You can target media to ask the right question to the right group of customers to get them engaged.

Myth 2: People who are selling are doing us a disservice.

Truth: "Salespeople" are generally good. Doesn't mean you want to have holiday meals with them, but a good salesperson listens and facilitates an even-handed buying decision on your part. They are doing you a service.

We have all purchased something—you probably did today—that made you feel good. You might feel better about yourself in the right article of clothing; see yourself as a good negotiator because you got a great deal; or believed you finally discovered the perfect electronics item with all the bells and whistles, constructed in a sleek, user-friendly, modern way. Provided he or she was courteous, the person (or entity) who led you to that proud purchase is most likely someone you appreciated at some level.

Bad salespeople exist. So what? So do bad singers. Move on.

Myth 3: Products advertised through infomercials are junk.

Truth: Most infomercials you see consistently are only on air because they are successfully selling to satisfied customers. The more identified the maker of the product, the higher your chances of having a successful experience. Known brand makers rely on direct response primarily to describe the value of products that can't be fully understood in 30 seconds or less. The lesson in buyer-beware comes typically from new people in the marketplace. And, frankly, the old adage applies: If it sounds too good to be true, it probably is. Do you believe you can look 30 years younger in 30 seconds? Lose 50 pounds in 30 days? Make $50,000 in your first 30 days in real estate? Those are probably not going to happen for the highly unmotivated. But no more shame on them than on a soda manufacturer that claims to make you thinner and sexier, a car maker with a "green car" toting 2 engines and 3,000 pounds of lithium batteries that promises to makes you ecologically sound, or a light beer that enhances your masculinity and sex appeal. There are bogus messages in every form of advertising. There are also true ones.

We believe that the only bad sales pitch is one that results in fraud or an unhappy customer. Time generally causes bad products, bad salespeople, and bad pitches to fall into early extinction. Sometimes products truly do make our lives easier and keep us happier. If you think that's untrue, do what we did as kids: live without a remote control. Get up and change the channel manually for a week!

Myth 4: People who are advertising to us are trying to manipulate us into making decisions that are bad for us.

Truth: Advertisers certainly are attempting to engage in business with you; what you see as manipulation may be considered by the target audience as identification. Any advertisement is ultimately seeking to make a business profitable. Profit drives jobs, growth, and innovation, and is the base of all proven economies. The vast majority of companies are selling good products in ethical ways.

The less you need a product, or the less actual differences there are between one brand and another, the more emotionally targeted, celebrity-dependant, or humorous advertising gets. That is because the products do not have their own unique selling proposition, or USP. The advertising tries to be the differentiator. This tends to fall most often into strict brand advertising, and the only real jab I'll take at this kind of advertising. I actually enjoy the genius creativity of Madison Avenue. At the end of the day, my wife is just as beautiful if she wears Revlon, MAC, or Max Factor. As for me, I can hit any brand of golf ball 275 yards—albeit into the woods. The difference between excellent products is usually marginal.

Understanding where this prejudice comes from, it seems that the modern marketplace is making valuable strides in eroding away this behavior. Most advertisers are in business because they believe they have found a better solution for a segment or larger group of us. The cost and competition of media, messaging, and customer acquisition is fueling an unprecedented drive toward direct response advertising as in no time prior. The vast majority of companies are well intentioned, ethical, and caring. You cannot afford in this day and age to say, "Our product appeals to everyone" then shotgun a message in hopes of landing business. That's a stupid waste of money. There are just too many messages out there pounding the audience.

Face it: You trust big corporations. It goes against our grain, but we believe in Ford, Gerber, Pfizer, even Bank of America. Think about it: All these companies have had some measure of product failure, legal problems, and embarrassment, but these same companies all have rebounded, have retained share value, and moved forward. Why? Because we know that their individual brands have historically done more good than bad. Truth be told, most products in the world are good, safe, and experienced positively by us. The hundreds of thousands of iconic world brands are a testament to this. We sit in focus groups routinely. Ask a consumer group about a new product and they will inevitably ask, "Who makes it?" or "Who's it by?" Which is another way of saying there are hundreds and hundreds of large corporations we trust. If a product is manufactured by them, we consider that a positive endorsement.

Where the Federal Trade Commission (FTC) and Federal Communication Commission (FCC) see potential harm being done, they willfully step in and regulate. They are very diligent. Remember saying goodbye to Joe Camel? These agencies know how to make an example out of the "bad eggs" and bad advertising. They police the industry with a very smart public "herding" system of controls. That's why we as consumers have them represent us.

Myth 5: Corporations want to sell anybody anything. Regardless of who you are, just buy!

Truth: This ties closely to the previous discussion, but there was a day and age when this was completely true. Iconic American brands like Coke, Levi's, Converse, Wonder Bread, and Chevrolet were built on the principle that nearly everybody needed and could use their products. That is not the case anymore. Simply spraying your marketing message and hoping that will translate into sales is going the way of the dinosaur. It is simply too expensive and too risky to just brand advertise. Modern intelligent advertisers must measure their budgets and correlate them to actual sales. Direct response is measureable, quantifiable, and trackable. You must be able to find your customers and target them in all forms of media, then get them to take an action toward your product. We produce metrics that garner grins all the way from the factory floor to the IT department to finance. We see it daily as more and more Fortune 500 type companies call us and ask us to consult.

The fragmentation of brands has driven the desire for unique identity for the consumer. There used to be a Levi's customer who represented all denim. Today, the consumer chooses you. Who *the customer* identifies with within the denim category is the key. Brand advertising leaves corporations trying to nudge the market share lines. Wrangler, Levi's, Calvin Klein, Ralph Lauren, and more battle this war daily. Our hope is to teach you the basics of how to ignore those lines and create whole new niches you can dominate. We want you to see yourself as creating a new business, to sneak in at night and defeat Goliath then force him to pay you to restore his empire. Harvard Business School has a term for this; it's called "FU money." It's exactly what we helped do for OxiClean, the George Foreman Grill, and Sonicare.

The Geeks Inherit
the Earth

A revolution has occurred in our lifetime, one that anyone born in the 1950s or 1960s would tell you was unthinkable to them. There was this whole section of culture that we had consistently ignored, even made fun of—the nerds. Those guys in math class, in the computer lab, in the chess club, with pocket protectors, calculators with way too many buttons, and those stupid plaid shirts. Well, while we were all acting cool, hanging out on or under the bleachers, the geeks inherited the earth.

They sure showed us. What they saw that none of the rest of us did was the potential of the phone, the television, and electronics to connect us. They saw the capability of the personal computer to connect us further, when the rest of us would have sworn that computers were the supreme tool of isolationism. We were wrong. The nerds were right. The value of personal computing, even beyond that of television, will be what our "age" will be known for, long after we are dust.

The catalyst this put in motion has folded our reality inside out. Beyond the Dick Tracy comic book characters of our childhood, with their wristwatch phones, today we enjoy a world where we can set up a global conference call, read an e-mail, text a message, and broadcast streaming live video, all while we're holding a cup of coffee in our other hand.

Today's consumer is media saturated—television, radio, phones, subway banners, e-mail pop-ups. The average consumer filters through more than 40,000 attempts to grab his or her attention every week. The consumer's mind has to sort and decide what to key into and what to ignore. Yet we are also constantly looking for products that help us live better lives. How will consumers find advertising that is relevant to them, and how will advertisers align their crosshairs on the perfect potential customer?

Think about what this has done just in the past five years to your ability as a consumer to filter messages. You are so barraged with branded media messaging that you can almost completely ignore it.

Assuming you were an advertiser in 1970, there was narrow enough television media space that if you found your way onto one of the three big networks, your product would be seen. It would garner customers. You just had to belly up to the bar and pay the piper for airtime. Blast the message and you were a "brand." That flat-out doesn't exist today, except on very rare occasions. Want to get everybody's eyeballs? Fork over $1 million for 15 seconds of Super Bowl ad space—and you better be *very* good.

In the same era, magazine titles ran only into the hundreds. That number is literally in the tens of thousands today. The vast majority are guaranteed sales. Do you know what that means? The publisher prints 10 million copies and places them on racks; the retailer pays only for inventory that actually sells. Why? Magazine revenue is based on "circulation." The more the publishers print and distribute, the more they can charge for the ads. "Ten million in circulation" starts to become real questionable.

In the early years of television there were a handful of very successful products and marketers, among them Alvin Eicoff's Flypel insect repellant and his rodent eradicator, D-Con; Lou Wunderman's introduction of the Time-Life music brand; and Arnold Morris's Kitchen Gourmet. By the end of the 1950s, the FTC had shut down the long-form infomercial format as a protection to the consumer from unscrupulous marketers.

From this point forward to the mid-1980s, there was no meaningful form of direct response television. Then came Ronald Reagan.

In 1984, spurred by the attempts of marketers to once again sell on television, President Reagan helped influence the FCC to remove the restrictions that limited the number and length of advertisements TV stations could show in an hour. This deregulation is held as the moment the modern infomercial genie was let out of the bottle.

The coincidence of the era that began in the late 1980s and continues through today was the result of a confluence of a number of rising trends, starting with cable television. The explosion of cable television made more airtime more available in more places. Infomercials gave cable stations programming to run in their off-hours. An inventory of shows that paid to be on the air truly helped small cable networks make it, to break even, or better. What were 10 or 12 cable networks in 1985 has increased exponentially to more than 500 channels in most markets today. Paid programming remains an important part of the profit model for most networks.

The next really important facet to fall in line with direct response has been the advent of personal computing and the explosion of the Internet. The ability to drive a consumer to a web portal to purchase a product was easy to see up front. In 2003, about 15 percent of purchases for our clients were coming from television advertising, which was driving web purchases. Today, we are seeing many clients averaging 50 to 60 percent of their DR sales coming from the web. We even have campaigns that rely 100 percent on web sales, particularly for clients that rely entirely on short-form direct response.

The next area of our industry where we're starting to see germination take place is mobile device marketing. In the coming years we will routinely accept pings and messages from marketers and retailers; many already do. This is already a hugely profitable industry in Asia, particularly Japan. The manifestation of this in the United States will be through messaging you request from cybervendors you approve, and from traditional retail marketers that want your business. As you know by the banner ads you get on Facebook, Yahoo!, or MSN, there is a cyberintelligence out there paying attention to every place you go, every keystroke you make, and every preference you select. You can fully expect that as a self-selected member of a Starbucks preferred customer program, for example, you will be pinged as you come within physical range of a store, and receive a notification of an incentive to stop by and order now!

Why Is Direct Response a Great Value?

It would be rational to expect that with the expansion of these media channels, both online and through digital cable television, advertising rates would plummet, due to increased inventory. That is not the case. If anything, media rates seem to rise higher and higher year after year. This has been a real danger to companies that rely on brand advertising alone. The costs of advertising have only escalated. The channels of media distribution have grown exponentially. The advent of mass-niche and micro-niche marketing is upon us.

Brand advertising is paid for and scheduled up front. That is, the traditional agency provides an exact map of where and when spots will run, along with the associated costs, at the beginning of a quarter. The advertiser pays a premium to be in a certain time slot. Here's an example. If you want to sell your Fancy Brand golf balls during the Masters Tournament, at the beginning of the quarter, you might purchase a slot during the second commercial break. The network is in the business of bidding up those spots as high as possible. Let's say that the value for this example ends up being $100,000. The network can report to the agency that it anticipates making X number of impressions for that slot.

Direct response media is *remnant time*. That means it is possible during that same golf tournament that some of the available ad space went unsold. This time often ends up in the remnant market, where it may be bid for by direct response media companies. Thus, it is completely feasible that right next to the $5,000 golf ball spot, HD Vision Sunglasses will run a one-minute spot for which it paid only $1,000.

The unfortunate thing for Fancy Brand golf balls is that the company may never truly know how many golf ball sales that particular spot generated. HD Vision, on the other hand, will know exactly how many glasses it sold; due to a unique 1-800 number and a spike in web traffic, HD will have statistical data. Better than that, HD will have a new customer or inquiry in its database for future marketing, and thus be connected to a real, live, breathing customer. Suddenly, HD Vision Sunglasses looks like a pretty smart business venture.

This example may seem overblown. It is not. We recently had a client purchase a 30-minute time slot that was intended to run nationally after an hour gap beyond the scheduled end of a professional golf event—a slot that normally is very cheap, as viewers are usually long gone. However, the event ran into a playoff and preempted scheduled programming. Suddenly our client's pain relief product had a clean lead-in from the PGA Tour event. We now had underpaid substantially for this national commercial time. The phone and web site exploded with activity. Resulting sales were astronomical, and clearly attributable to this particular airing.

The key differentiators between traditional brand and direct response are multiple. The major ones you need to know from day one are:

- Brand advertising relies on traditional measures, including reach, frequency, penetration, and impressions. It spends a large amount of money to "spray" a message, which hopefully increases sales that are measured over the long haul of a campaign, often stretching into quarters after actual ads run. The measurement of success is often unclear in real time.

- Short-form direct response relies on general viewer demographics and instant response. The media cost is a fraction of brand rates. The actual placement of the ads is determined by the network to fill otherwise unfilled ad space, keeping the costs lower. The ads make an offer that drives a consumer to take an action, usually calling a 1-800 number or visiting a web site. Each media outlet has a devoted phone number that makes the response attributable to the consumer response. Direct response agencies can monitor and calculate metrics, virtually in real time, to measure the efficiency of their spots.

These key differentiators are what allow us at our agency to constantly move and adjust our clients' media schedules to maximize profit potential on a weekly basis.

Why Doesn't Everyone Try Direct Response?

Ron and I scratch our heads every day over this one. Frankly, we have to believe there are some pretty simple reasons. First, there is a stigma associated with direct response, particularly from those who do not understand the actual power of it. The assumption is that the style of spots that are frequently the most memorable can be considered a little odd or "off the wall." ShamWow, Snuggie, and Ginsu knives are what most people think of when you say "infomercial" or "direct response." The pop culture icons personified by Billy Mays, Ron Popeil, and Vince the ShamWow guy typify the selling style most corporations are afraid of. It is called "yell and sell." It works, but you might not want your brand presented that way. We get that.

The truth is, as memorable as these folks are, they represent only a thin sliver of the personalities that represent brands in direct response. Many brands are currently represented by credible celebrities. They share sincere and direct approaches that fly in the face of the yell-and-sell pitchman. Think of Peggy Fleming for Hunter Fan Co., Jeff Gordon for DuPont, and Angie Harmon for Johnson & Johnson consumer products—all people we have worked with in the last few years.

The second reason for a lack of involvement in DR is predisposition and education. Most marketing executives are just ignorant of the process and the results direct response generates. As we mentioned earlier, there is no school that teaches the details and mechanics of this industry. This business is entrepreneurial. The people who created it are so busy making real money at it that they don't tend to stop to take teaching jobs that would undercut the action, excitement, and financial gain this business delivers. Probably the same reason Ted Turner isn't teaching communications at Atlanta Community College. If you have a master's degree in marketing from a prestigious school, you probably never learned about the true business genius of direct response; the industry is *that* new, relatively speaking. Hopefully, this book will give you the "toe in the water" you need to open up your mind to the possibilities of being an innovator within your company. Consider these stats resulting from the use of direct response marketing:

- Juiceman sales went from $0 to $75 million in only four years.
- OxiClean reached $200 million in the same time frame.
- Optiva Corporation, the makers of the Sonicare toothbrush, was number one on *Inc.* magazine's list of fastest-growing companies.

Our industry tends to grow organically, from two places. The first is individuals who invent products and have the dream to grow a company, big and fast. When they look for models of how to do it, inevitably they come across direct response and jump in. Why? Because direct response is advertising that pays for itself. These companies can create large media campaigns starting with few resources. The second is from chief marketing officers who were once with brands that were built through direct response. It seems that once these folks get the DR "bug," they tend to infect the corporations they go to later. Many of our clients come to us from a direct contact their marketing people have had with us over the years, and met through otherwise unrelated product launches.

It is also worth mentioning that there is still, and always will be, a place and value for brand product advertising. Direct response media inventory is growing, though still limited, due to the stronghold traditional brand advertising has on available airtime. Our industry benefits by the brand advertisers' rates. We are the yin to their yang. As long as advertisers pay traditional brand rates, there will be a financial benefit to our clients to participate in lower rates of direct response.

This being said, we still do not expect that brand advertising will disappear over time. Our industry products tend to hinge on something called a unique selling proposition (USP). The products that work best in DR typically provide some level of technological supremacy or some novelty or design innovation that makes them stand apart from previous products. Brand products are often so close to their competitors in terms of functionality, there is no USP. They end up standing on consumer identity alone. The difference between Coke and Pepsi, some would argue, is flavor. We would argue that the difference is how the consumer was driven by the advertising—you are either a Coke person or a Pepsi person. At the end of the day, they are both sugar and water. We'll discuss later how to create a USP so you can take advantage of direct response and get your customer to buy now.

What Is a Brand and Why Do I Need One?

We can already sense you rolling your eyes. Remember what we said in the beginning: If you assume you know everything, you know nothing. Don't skip this section; it might be the most important one in the book.

Ask 10 people to name an iconic brand and within the first 10 answers you will no doubt hear Kleenex, Nike, Q-tips, BAND-AID, and Coke. They are all correct—fabulous brands each one. Ask these same people why these products come to mind as a brand and they most likely will say some version of, "Because the name of the product has culturally taken the place of the object." When you need to clean your ears or remove makeup, you reach for a Q-tip. When a kid has the sniffles, Mom hands her a Kleenex. We don't go around asking for cotton swabs and disposable tissues. That's true; but that alone is not *brand*. Scott Tissue takes up its fair share of space at the grocery. House-brand swabs successfully compete at Target, Walmart, and Walgreens. Brand in our day and age has become something much more quantifiable. It has to do with market share and lineal feet in retail.

A *brand* is an identifiable entity, with consumer space measured in dollars. In our world, a good, growing brand disrupts the retail and e-commerce space of a larger company or creates new space in commerce. The goal of brand in this model is that eventually the larger company is forced to buy our brand at a premium, or risk the possibility that its competitor will do so. A *premium brand* is one that not only does that but that has a strong enough identified efficacy with the consumer such that, when attached to other brands, it will increase their value, their sales, and their profits. OxiClean is a terrific example of brand building and execution; we'll dive into that in a minute.

The best thing about our strategy for building a brand is that it comes up on the competitor so fast—as if from nowhere.

It's indefensible. It's truly the David and Goliath marketing model. The best part is that you can do it over and over and over again and the principles always work, every time.

Any smart entrepreneur comes to the table with two things: (1) an innovative idea, service, or product; (2) a business plan with an exit strategy. A significant amount of work we do is to create and execute incredible exit strategies for our clients. A powerful exit strategy has to do with *brand* as we define it—that is, market share plus lineal retail space.

The golden chalice of any new product is getting retail space in the places American consumers visit weekly. The grocery store, Target, Walmart, or a variety of category mass merchandisers, even some mom-and-pops and specialty stores like garden or automotive stores. The key question is: "How do I get on the shelves?"

This seems like a catch-22 for most companies. How do I get space without a huge advertising budget? If I get space, then it's guaranteed sale merchandise. That means if it doesn't sell, you have to take it back. Who is the buyer? How do I get a meeting? Where the hell is Bentonville, Arkansas (it's the location of Walmart's world headquarters), and why do I have to go there? Where am I going to get the money for a huge advertising campaign with no sales? What if the big company likes my idea so much it rips me off?

These questions can seem so daunting it makes most people stop before they start.

Let's talk in some detail about someone we did this for. There's a tremendous amount of learning to be gleaned from our experience with a pitchman named Billy Mays and a product called OxiClean. (I promise we'll get to the lessons we learned from the Juiceman, the George Foreman Grill, and the Sonicare toothbrush, which put us on the marketing map, but for the moment we need to flash past those roots of the late 1980s and early 1990s when we really had optimized our skills.)

Having recently brought a product called Quick n Brite off the county fair circuit and into homes, through the vehicle of an infomercial, Cesari Direct was riding high. We created direct sales of over $15 million in about 18 months. The product was placed in retail stores, where it remains today a staple in many homes.

Because of this success, in 1996 we were approached by a company called Orange Glo International. Max Appel and family owned a small company based in Denver that sold a product called OxiClean, an invention of their own they had been successfully selling at fairs for years and through a home shopping channel. They became aware of our work after Quick n Brite went from the same fairs to strong TV success.

The OxiClean product was extremely effective, had brilliant visual demonstrations, and was loved by everyone who used it. The only problem? Selling one $10 or $20 tub of this stuff to one customer at a time worked great at county fairs, but the time and energy of a traveling circus lifestyle was hard on the family. And once you deduct the cost of travel, hotels, a fair booth, plus the cost of manufacturing a product in your own factory, then divide the profit between a number of partners . . . well, imagine, it was just about more work than it was worth.

Max Appel had started to realize some easy sales on the home shopping network, using Billy Mays as the pitchman. This crystallized a bigger vision for reaching even more people through television. Max had seen with his own eyes through the success of Quick n Brite that we had a method to reach it. (There is a funny story that Max reminds me of every time I see him: We were both at an industry trade show and he and his son Joel were trying to get a meeting with me, and I kept refusing, not because I did not think they had a good product but because I felt there would be a conflict representing two household cleaning products. I kept saying no until my brother, Steve, who had a chance to meet with them briefly told me I needed to meet the OxiClean guys. We finally did get together, but Max likes to remind me that I almost passed on the OxiClean opportunity.)

The beginning of the OxiClean empire started very simply: We created a half-hour program relying on Max Appel's best presenter, pitchman Billy Mays. This was Mays's very first infomercial and the start of his hugely successful TV career. He did a simple demonstration that took a sphere of iodized water and turned it clear with the magic stain-erasing power of OxiClean. The image of that disgusting reddish-brown water turning crystal clear in seconds, plus the booming voice—"Powered by the air you breathe, fueled by the water you drink"—and we literally had magic in a bottle. Mays then walked through a home eradicating what would be thought of as one disastrous stain after the next. He used this little tub of OxiClean to restore thousands of dollars in furnishings, curtains, and clothing, in seconds. He gave the product meaning.

But wait—there's more.

Proving the incredible efficacy of OxiClean was not enough. We had to give it value. Certainly, saving thousands in repair and replacement was valuable; and Mays proved that a little went a long way. Next came the offer.

Recall earlier, we mentioned that part of the value of direct response is its ability to avoid the costs associated with traditional supply chain mechanics. When you start cutting out the middlemen, you can afford to give the customer a lot more. We did. First Mays established the value of the tub at $19.95. Then he doubled its size, making the offer worth $39.90. Next he added spray bottles, cleaning utensils, and cloths, all the while showing the value of each. By the time he was finished, he had an offer that was worth $80, which you could only get if you called to buy now. The phone lines went nuts.

I remember coming in the Monday after the first weekend the show tested—I had to have the numbers rerun three times.

We could not believe the overwhelming response to this product and to the big, fun, relatable bear of a man who sold it. Remember, this was in 1996, the pre-Internet commerce days. One hundred percent of the volume was phone orders. We had lightning in a bottle—or tub, as the case may be. One dollar in ad spending returned $3 to $4 in revenue.

That is not the end of the story; just the beginning, in fact. In subsequent months and first years, we did show after show, almost 15 long-form shows, and then spot after spot featuring combinations of the entire Orange Glo product line: OxiClean, KABOOM tub and tile cleaner, Orange Glo furniture polish, Orange Clean oven degreaser, and many more. The alchemy of success was perfect. We had the right guy, who could get your attention. We had the right product; this stuff worked. And we had a low enough cost-of-goods and distribution model that allowed the company to constantly reinvest in product development and growth. The true power of direct response advertising is that it pays for itself. This enabled a small start-up company to spend huge advertising dollars leading to increased revenues, brand awareness, and retail distribution. OxiClean was more than a great product, it was a great ingredient; and looking at it as such was the secret to building the true brand with the connective tissue to penetrate retail, widen with individual SKUs, and disrupt the sales of larger competitors.

In the coming years, OxiClean's active ingredient was put into a variety of products that we could brand with the "Oxi" prefix. There was a variety of tub sizes, packets, and, eventually, laundry-specific products, sprays, and stain removers. Max Appel did not have to call the retailers and beg them for shelf space; they called him! What started as one SKU of OxiClean in retailers turned into a complete line of products that shoved their way into grocery stores and mass merchants around the globe.

OxiClean had become one of the biggest brands in cleaning, in a matter of five years. Sales were in the neighborhood of $200 million. Think about that. Looking back on it, it almost feels like an out-of-body experience to live that kind of growth. The Appels worked very hard for many years to build their business, and the power of direct response made theirs an iconic brand almost overnight.

But wait—there's still more.

Now the Appels' company had true brand power—remember, the combination of lineal feet and market share. Over the short and meteoric rise, Orange Glo International was gobbling up shelf space like PAC-MAN. People noticed. Those people are called *retail merchandisers*. They are the folks you see in the grocery store aisles in blue oxford shirts with shelf schematics in their hand. (A *shelf schematic* maps the exact location of products at retail, which can determine the penny profit of retailers.) The power to decide what goes where in any store is one of the last factors that control consumer purchase habits. In many places, those who draw the maps win. When retail merchandisers report back to their corporation that new items are encroaching on shelf space and real estate, all hell breaks loose. Really.

The great news for Orange Glo International was that it had caused a considerable disruption to sales in one of the most loyal and profitable consumer segments—cleaning and laundry. The big players include Procter & Gamble, Lever Brothers, Clorox, Church & Dwight, Arm & Hammer, Dial, and Henkel—all huge corporations with long histories and deep pockets. We cannot tell you what went on behind the scenes in 2006, or who the specific bidders were, but in the end, the Appel family sold the business to Church & Dwight, the English conglomerate that owns Arm & Hammer Brands. They walked away with a check well north of $300 million—that's cash, no stock swap, no slow payout. Ka-ching. The best part was, it couldn't happen to nicer people. The good news for you? There's no reason to prevent you from duplicating their model. I know firsthand because I lived it before the Appels.

They Don't Teach This in College

Rick's Story

B efore we move on to examine more of the big product hits in my career, I'm going to invite you into my thought process. (If you want to skip some of the historical background and just get to the nuts and bolts of this powerful marketing model please go to Chapter 10.)

The following is my story on how I got started in the infomercial business.

I grew in knowledge and experience as a result of who I am and where I came from. I'm sharing my background with you in case you can glean any insights or make any observations from it that you can use to your advantage.

I've always been a big believer in selling through education or information. I know that if you provide consumers with the necessary information, they'll draw their own conclusions in favor of the product. Maybe I like this approach so much because this was how I succeeded in my first "real" sales job, selling suntan lotion, pool-side in Daytona Beach. My approach has always been to explain why the product is necessary *and* how it accomplishes the desired result. I focus on the *benefits* of the product, whether it's suntan lotion, a juicer, toothbrush, or laundry product. One way to accomplish this is using the problem/solution scenario: first explain what the problem is, then offer a solution. For example:

"Want to be healthier and live longer? Drink fresh juice!" (Juiceman)

"Want whiter teeth, a better dental checkup, and healthier teeth and gums? Get Sonicare!"

"Want to cook a hamburger to perfection in half the time? Get a George Foreman Grill!"

35

"Want to get grass or juice stains out of the kids' jeans? Use OxiClean, the antibleach!"

The problem/solution setup can be designed around almost anything. In a way it isn't much different from the approach I used to sell suntan lotion, years ago, on the pool deck.

The Pitch

In my experience, no matter what the product is, the best way to present it is to give people the information they need to make a buying decision. This information should be presented in a linear fashion, leading people to the action you want them to take. This is called the "pitch." The pitch includes anticipating potential questions that might pop into people's heads and answering as many of them as possible in the presentation.

Explain the problem, introduce a solution, resolve questions, then offer some testimony; organizing a presentation this way turns a complicated decision-making process into a common-sense deduction. Ideally, the viewer should think, "Why didn't someone think of this until now?" Common sense is how people decide whether or not to shell out their hard-earned cash on a product. Helping people find common-sense solutions has been an incredibly effective way of doing business for me over the years.

Build a brand starting with a great product that people need and that solves a problem; sell it with an honest, informative selling approach; make an irresistible offer; then give people the opportunity to order the product if they choose. It doesn't matter if the interaction is through TV, the web, or retail sales. Give customers their choice of how they want to buy. When people have a good experience making a decision, and are satisfied with the purchase, they feel good about the product and will tell other potential buyers, creating a snowball effect. This is a very simple formula, whereby the more people you expose to a direct response advertising campaign the more you will increase (exponentially!) the number of happy satisfied customers, not to mention your revenue.

My Story

I grew up playing catch, watching TV, and dreaming about the future in a small town in Westchester County, not far from White Plains, New York, called Valhalla. My father owned a small grocery store in the business center, across the street from the train station. My dad was also a butcher, so the family shop was known for its fresh meats, personal service, and free deliveries. This was 40 years before Amazon started doing the same thing. My four brothers and I all worked in the grocery store, stocking shelves and helping with the deliveries. It was truly a family business. My grandfather opened the store after he arrived in America from Italy. He worked in that store every day until he was 91 years old.

My grandfather taught me many valuable lessons. One is how good deeds can truly be rewarded in this life. One of my favorite stories is how this probably saved my father's life.

According to Grandpa, when Dad was a machine gunner in the infantry during World War II, he was supposed to be in the first wave of soldiers storming Omaha Beach in Normandy. The night before the landing was scheduled, my dad got called in to see the commanding officer. The major asked my dad, "Cesari, huh? Any relation to Cesari's in Vallhalla, New York?"

My Father answered, "Yes."

The major said, "Your father helped my family through the Depression by giving us groceries." Because of this the major moved my dad from the front lines—despite his protests. Instead of going in the first wave, Dad was now scheduled to land on the second day.

It was this small switch that probably saved my dad's life on that terrible day. And who's to say? Maybe my grandfather was absolutely right, that every small act of good or kindness influences what we get in life. Watching my father and grandfather, I saw with my own eyes how honesty, hard work, generosity, and customer service paid off. They taught me that the customer is always right.

This story also highlights how sound business values never really go out of style. The things my grandfather and father were telling me, about how to treat customers with respect, deeply influenced my approach to the direct response TV (DRTV) spots I developed much later.

From Real Estate to Infomercials

I was lucky: We moved just in time for me to start high school in our new town, Daytona Beach, Florida. I was able to go to Father Lopez High School. I was athletic and bursting with energy so I played football on my school's team; my senior year I played fullback and middle linebacker.

After high school, I went to Westminster College in New Wilmington, PA, and got a BS degree in biology. I also played on the college football team and won two national championships. Winning or succeeding has always been in my blood. After graduating college, in 1978, I wanted to take a break for a while so I moved back to Daytona.

I've always been practical, so when I returned to sunny Florida I started working in the two areas the beach is famous for. I became a pool lifeguard whose main duty was to sell tourists suntan lotion and a bartender at night. My mother was not happy with my career choices! A good portion of my income depended on how much suntan lotion I could sell in a day. Earning a percentage of every bottle was a great motivator for me. This was my first experience with direct selling. It was here that I learned to adapt and refine my sales pitch to reap the best results.

Some of the things I learned selling suntan lotion direct to the consumer still hold true for products I sell today. Present the problem (how do I get a great tan?), offer a solution (the Hawaiian Tropic suntan lotion I was selling), and explain the benefits and why my product was better than anything else in the market. Presto! People would buy.

I knew I was not going to do this work forever, so I also was constantly reading books about how to improve my life. I read two types of books: those on how to make money in real estate, and self-help/motivational books. At the time, popular motivational titles were *Think and Grow Rich* by Napoleon Hill, *The Magic of Thinking Big* by Richard Schwartz, *The Success System That Never Fails* by W. Clement Stone, and *The Power of Positive Thinking* by Norman Vincent Peale. These people were the Tony Robbins of their time. Their basic message was: "What you think about all the time you can manifest in your life." What I was thinking about was: "How can I get rich?"

Of the how-to-make money books, I read mostly ones that focused on buying real estate, by authors such as Mark Haroldsen, Albert Lowry, and in particular, Robert Allen's famous book on investing called *Nothing Down*. These books gave me a specific plan on how to make money by investing in real estate. After reading them I decided to get a real estate broker's license and get into the business.

The people who wrote the real estate books also offered live seminars. I attended one in Orlando by a man named Tom Vu, who taught participants how to buy distressed or foreclosed property. It was the Vu seminar that changed the whole direction of my life.

Vu was doing something different that was more interesting to me. He focused his approach, as I said, on buying distressed property, otherwise known as foreclosures. This meant that most of the properties could be acquired at below-market rates. The benefit was that you could sell them right away and make money immediately! No waiting for months or years to make your first dollar. No borrowing money to tear out plaster and replace it with drywall, to hire plumbers and roofers, and to oversee the reconstruction. The Vu method was quick and straight to the point. The reason I liked it was that it was a unique selling proposition, or USP, for marketing his seminars nationwide.

I managed to learn enough at that initial seminar that I could apply in my real life. Two weeks after taking Vu's seminar I went out and found a house in foreclosure and just about to be lost to the bank. I made a deal to give the homeowner $1,000 and then take over the loan. I then contracted to buy the house for $12,000. I immediately turned around and advertised it for sale. Within days I got an offer. Someone wanted to buy it for $24,000—before I had even closed on my purchase. I ended up bringing both contracts to the title company and did a simultaneous closing. Without putting up any money or taking out any loans, I walked away with a little over $10,000—for two weeks' work. That was a lot of money at the time. I thought, *this is great!* I wanted to do more.

At this point all I wanted to do was buy and sell more houses. But one other important thing I did after completing my first real estate transaction was to contact the leading business magazine in the state, called *Florida Trend*. It had run a major story about Vu, which really boosted his credibility and helped get his struggling seminar business off the ground. This early lesson taught me the value of PR, the impact it could have on the product or service you are marketing.

I moved to Orlando and over the next three years, I helped build the Vu seminar business into the largest in the country. He became much wealthier from his seminars than from the real estate investing he was doing. This is also how I learned about the power of DRTV.

In 1982, Ronald Reagan deregulated television, allowing more advertisements per hour. Previously, TV stations were limited to selling only eight minutes each hour. After deregulation, they could sell the entire hour as an ad, if they wanted to. The first people to truly take advantage of this were the real estate seminar promoters, people like Ed Beckley out of Fairfield, Iowa. He had a program called *The Millionaire Maker*, which was hugely successful at the time. The one that had the most impact on me, though, featured the aforementioned Robert Allen, out of Salt Lake City. He had a tremendously successful seminar business. (Carlton Sheets, who created one of the most successful, longest-running infomercials ever, got his start as a pitchman for Allen's "Nothing Down" seminars.)

I liked this show because it was done in a documentary style. It motivated the viewers and actually educated them about the concept of real estate investing. It featured interviews with several bestselling authors, and was just a classier-than-average show. I later used this style and format for some of my more successful infomercials.

I produced the very first infomercials to market the Vu seminars, and did all the media buying. This is how I learned the infomercial business firsthand. I wrote, produced, and edited a one-hour documentary-style show called *Secrets of Success*.

One of the biggest reasons most infomercials do not work is that viewers do not believe what they are hearing and seeing. The best way to overcome this is by establishing credibility. One way to do this is to have a host that people admire and trust. After a long search, I hired a well-respected character actor who exuded trustworthiness, named Mason Adams.

In the 1960s, Adams was a ubiquitous voiceover actor in television commercials, most notably for Chiffon Margarine and Crest toothpaste—"Helps stop cavities before they start." He was also the voice of the Smucker's Preserves television commercials. You may remember him saying, "With a name like Smucker's, it has to be good!"

Adams was most famous for his role as Managing Editor Charlie Hume on the *Lou Grant* television series, which aired from 1977 until 1982. He also routinely played bankers, executives, and even on occasion, the president. This archetype was entirely unique in the infomercial and DRTV business at the time. Adams was the most credible host we could find. Everybody trusted him.

This use of a credible actor to host the shows and be the spokesperson for the products was a tactic I employed over and over in some of my most successful infomercials. Another good example is Richard Dysart, who hosted my Sonicare infomercial. He played the part of Leyland McKenzie, the head of the firm on the popular TV series *L.A. Law*.

I chose to create informative television shows that discussed how viewers could learn something and make money themselves. This educational or informative approach was new.

Secrets of Success was a hit with TV viewers. Vu's seminar business eventually developed into the largest in the country at the time, ultimately bringing together about 13,000 people during a single week in Los Angeles.

I continued to do this for about two years; I left when it became clear that Vu and I didn't really see eye to eye on ethics. It was after I left that he started producing sleazy infomercials featuring yachts and scantily clad women to promote his seminars.

The interesting thing about this early period in infomercial history is that it launched many of the original infomercial pioneers who have run some of the biggest direct response agencies or companies in the business: Ed Beckley, whom I mentioned earlier, was based in Fairfield, Iowa, now home to Tim Hawthorne of Hawthorne Direct; Paul Simon was based in Phoenix, Arizona, the home of "Twin Star"; Mike Levey, best known for hosting *Amazing Discoveries*; and Don Lewis Advertising, in Los Angeles, which promoted both Albert Lowry and Tony Hoffman. My good friend and very successful infomercial writer Mark Scarpacci worked at Don Lewis in the 1980s; one of his current shows you might have seen is for Hip Hop Abs.

Things have changed since the early days of the real estate seminar business. Yet it was through these formative experiences that I learned, mostly through trial and error, how to sell. I learned not just how to create a pitch but also the importance of establishing credibility with the audience. I learned about public relations, media buying, and making television shows. I even learned how to set up and put on successful seminars. Really, this is where I started learning what I needed to know to create successful long-term direct marketing campaigns. Things operated a whole lot differently then than they do in today's DRTV business. But these are the experiences that contributed to the later success of the Juiceman, Sonicare, George Foreman Grills, Momentus Golf, OxiClean, and Rug Doctor.

How to Make a Million

In 1986, I moved from Orlando to Seattle to start my own business. My old college friend Dale Hofmann was doing pretty well as a boat broker out in Seattle. He brokered fishing boats and even fished for salmon and halibut every summer in Alaska. One afternoon when we spoke on the phone I told him about an idea I had, to turn a book I'd read, *How to Make $1,000,000 in the Stock Market Automatically!* by Robert Lichello, into an infomercial.

Dale offered to invest $10,000 to put together the infomercial. Even in 1986 dollars this was a tight budget. I contacted Lichello and arranged for him to tape an inexpensive infomercial in a live talk show format. We used the local public television station studio to save money.

Producing the show put me back about $7,000 of the $10,000 Dale sent me. I used the outstanding $3,000 for airtime, on what was then the Tempo cable network.

After my work for the "How to Make a Million" project was essentially done, I had nothing to occupy my time while I waited to see if the show would make any money. I took Dale up on his invitation to go fishing with him in Alaska.

At the time, halibut fishing regulations were strictly controlled. The entire fleet was allotted an open time for long-line halibut fishing—say, 48 hours over June first and second. Rain or shine, the allotted time was the allotted time: You had to go fishing to make the payments on your boat. Commercial fishermen are a tough lot, just like they appear on the TV show *Deadliest Catch*. In fact, where the Alaskan king crabs come from, in the Bering Sea near the Aleutian Islands, is the area we fished. Dale and I joined his regular crewmates, and we spread out over two ships. I, two crewmen, and the captain were on the small 50-footer. Dale and the bulk of the crew stayed on the much larger 80-footer. (Maybe they knew something I did not!).

Even though I was young and in relatively good shape, I was definitely out of my element. After all, less than 20 hours earlier I had climbed onto a plane in sunny Florida. We set out on flat seas in 60-degree temperatures. As we laid our miles and miles of lines, the seas grew rougher. Before I knew what was really happening, we were in 60-mile-an-hour winds, with huge waves breaking everywhere. We'd gone beyond rough seas to something much worse; something darker. Our smaller ship was being tossed around like a toy boat. But for a while we were holding our own in the storm.

That is, until the engine cut out. When we lost power, we really started getting thrown around. We took some full-on hits while the captain was below trying to get the motor up and running. The rest of us hung on for dear life and tried to catch sight of the big ship. When the captain didn't reappear after quite a long time, the other crewman got edgy and went to check on him. He came back up screaming for help to drag out the captain, who was unconscious. Apparently he had fallen prey to fumes or hit his head.

After we managed to get the captain out of danger, we donned our survival suits and radioed the big ship to come tow us. Our motor was dead and wasn't coming back to life anytime soon. After an hour's worth of heaving and tossing, we finally managed to successfully catch the line the crew on the bigger ship had been throwing to us over and over again. What a relief it was to feel the ship towing us. At last, we were heading for safety.

But we were dragged only about a hundred yards before the line snapped. The big ship keeled around and we started the process all over again of throwing out and trying to catch a line in 20-foot crests. About an hour later we managed to catch and secure the steel cable they sent out this time. By now, we'd gotten dangerously close to the crags and cliffs of the islands. With no power of our own to steer clear of the rocks, the tow cable really was our life saver.

We started moving again, and this time kept moving beyond the first few seconds. Everyone let out a sigh of relief. Almost at that instant, however, at about 500 yards out, the cable snapped again, setting us adrift once more, off the rocky coast in blasting seas. At this point, with our captain now conscious but still groggy, the three of us tried to rationalize what would be the wise course of action: to abandon ship or to stay aboard. Which choice would give us a better chance of survival?

One more radio conversation with the captain of the 80-footer put our debate to rest. He and I decided to try to get the boats as close to one another as possible so the four of us could jump from our ship to theirs, and have a better chance of making it. The waves continued to crash erratically, allowing us no rhythm by which we could time our leap of faith. I managed to make it over the railing and onto the big ship, followed by the still-groggy captain. One more to go.

As the last man leapt toward us, the big ship struck the abandoned ship so hard we were all shaken. Had he waited an instant longer he would have been smashed. Had he jumped sooner, we would have been beyond his reach. The final crewman had made it. With everyone safely on board we headed into port, very happy to be alive!

Once ashore and patched up and dried out, I decided to phone the telemarketing company we had hired to take the calls that would come in from the broadcast of the Lichello infomercial. One of the best feelings in the infomercial business is checking the results after the first weekend of media testing. How well a program does in a limited number of airings tells you whether you have a winner worth millions, or you need to go back to the drawing board and start from scratch. We had spent $4,000 on media and generated $12,000 in sales. This is known as a "three-to-one" return, or a "huge success," in the industry.

While Dale and I had been busy fighting for our lives, the seeds of that first clear million were being planted. At the time, the earliest cable incarnation of the 24-hour news channel was the Financial News Network, which of course was the perfect forum for our show and our product. The "How to Make a Million Dollars" show ended up being a success.

Here is another lesson I will never forget: Do not assume that because you were successful in one business you will automatically be successful in another. I took some of the money I made from the success of the Lichello infomercial and used it to buy a telemarketing company in Seattle. I soon found out that running a telemarketing company was vastly different from marketing products on TV. I cut my losses and got back to what I do best: marketing products. It was 1997, and

I started selling a weight-loss product called Nu-Day through television. We sold almost $18 million worth in the next year and a half.

The inventor and eventual spokesperson for the Nu-Day weight loss product was Dr. Jeffrey Bland. Bland has a PhD in nutritional biochemistry, has published dozens of articles in the top scientific journals, and at one time ran the Linus Pauling Research Lab. You could not find a more credible, knowledgeable, and well-spoken person to host the show. This is one of the reasons it was so successful.

It was Bland who first got me interested in health, nutrition, and alternative medicine. He introduced me to Dr. Joe Pizzorno, who at the time was president of Bastyr University in Seattle. I spent three years on the board of directors there and learned a lot about health and nutrition—"You are what you eat"—and how certain foods can affect your health. This turned out to be a huge advantage when it came to marketing my next big success.

It was during this time that I met both David and Ellen Hofmann who are still with me at Cesari Direct. David is a partner and vice president of media, and Ellen runs our accounting department.

CHAPTER
4

Juicing for Dollars

You never know exactly what about a situation, a product, or a project is going to be the "one thing" that answers the nagging question or solves the outstanding riddle. It could be anything, from a comment overheard at a dinner party to something you find in the research. The "one thing" that suddenly makes all the other aspects of an issue fall into place and become manageable could be absolutely anything.

That's why I've taken the approach of sharing the evolution of my most important projects as they developed. I could easily just say, "I did this and this, and—voila!—it all worked." But that isn't the way real insights and realizations happen. No one ever developed his or her own dish by only following the recipe. It takes owning the ideas and applying them to your own situation to stimulate true learning.

As I wandered the expanse of the Seattle Coliseum's annual kitchen show in 1988, I noted a particularly popular pitchman doing a demonstration. I could sense how his charisma was affecting the dozen or so people around him—they were mesmerized. That man was Jay Kordich.

While Kordich was indeed captivating, his consummate skill as a salesman wasn't the only thing that grabbed my attention. He also was *teaching*—teaching people the nutritional benefits of drinking fresh juices. I'd been "into" health and nutrition myself for quite a while and I was always on the lookout for easier ways to make truly nutritional foods. In the mid-1980s, the health and nutrition boom was just starting, and the Pacific Northwest was the epicenter of both nutrition and alternative health care.

Before meeting Kordich I was already juicing as part of a healthy lifestyle. So when I did finally meet him that afternoon

in Seattle, I personally understood the incredible health benefits of juicing.

I took the time to chat with Kordich and find out more
about his product. I learned that he and his wife, Linda, were
owners and operators, organizing the whole juice machine
business by themselves. It was a mom-and-pop operation in
the truest sense. They had found a supplier of high-quality
juice machines, and traveled as a couple from kitchen shows
to state fairs demonstrating the product in the expo booths.

I asked if we could meet later at my office in Seattle, to see
if we could make a deal. My partners at the time did not want
to move forward with the project, however, because they were
concerned about how we would deal with repairing defective
juice machines. (Their objection taught me a valuable lesson:
that it is really easy to erect obstacles to success if you want to.)
Consequently, we decided not to do anything at the time, and
during the course of the year my partners and I decided to go
our separate ways.

About a year or so later I found myself at loose ends. In the
spring of 1989, I finally had time and the inclination to track
down Kordich and think more seriously about his product and
how I could help. As I learned later, just as I was trying to
find him, he'd hired his good friend, Jack Lee, as a business
advisor. Kordich and Lee were in the process of searching for
someone to launch an infomercial for Kordich's juice machine.
This is an example of where serendipity and good timing come
into play.

There are no rules or methods for getting serendipity to work
for you, except to take action on intuitive ideas that "stick."
An idea can become noticeably "sticky" in several ways. One
is when you keep thinking about it. If an idea or thought keeps
popping into your head over and over again, even if it doesn't
seem to have anything to do with what you're currently working on, pay attention to it.

Another way serendipity may happen is if the subject just keeps popping up all over the place. Let's say I file away the juice machine idea. Then, a few months later, I read a memoir of a great athlete who mentions juicing. Perhaps a few weeks after that I catch a snippet of something on the news about commercial juice products being mostly sugar water, as opposed to actually being nutritious. Then a week or two later, I'm cleaning up my office and organizing my files and I stumble across the card Jay Kordich handed me months ago. All of these pieces get me thinking about juicing, about what's available to the average consumer, and about Kordich's entertaining demonstration.

When I did finally get in touch with Kordich I was disappointed to find out that he and Lee had been negotiating with the Dave Del Dotto Group, a very successful TV and real estate firm. They were close to signing a contract with them to develop a direct television campaign. It also just so happened that Kordich and Lee were coming to Seattle, where I happened to live at the time (and still do). Because we had hit it off on a personal level, Kordich and Lee invited me to sit down with them while they were in town.

There's another important element to this story to take note of: When Kordich and Lee invited me to chat, I wasn't in any way prepared. At the time I had no organization, no company, and no business behind me at all. I was by myself, on my own; just a guy with a few successes and a lot of ideas. Dave Del Dotto, on the other hand, was all over television. He had a big telemarketing setup and a huge support system. I did not care. I saw this situation as a great opportunity and wanted to get involved any way I could.

As human beings, as people in a one-on-one way, Kordich and I really connected. The two of us discovered that, philosophically, we were in tune, especially from a health and nutrition perspective. We were both interested in improving the quality of people's lives, in helping them live in healthier, more vibrant ways. Both of us also were interested in much more than simply making money from this product. The goal of making money was never our sole intention. We made a simple agreement.

The Power of PR

To get this project up and running, I founded JM Marketing, with my brother, Steve, in 1989. This company eventually evolved into Trillium Health Products, which marketed the Juiceman juicer and the Breadman Breadmaker, as well as lots of educational books, tapes, and videos. I actually drew up the marketing plan that we followed on a napkin (which I still have), and in a little over three years, sales reached $75 million.

There is a funny story on how we actually got started. We finalized our deal at the end of May 1989, and the very first appearance we booked for Kordich was on the *Richard Bey Show*, on WWOR-TV in Secaucus, NJ. WWOR was one of the first superstations, which meant it broadcasted beyond the New York City market. Richard Bey was a local TV personality who hosted a morning talk show. Kordich and Bey hit it off on the air and ended up doing a 20-minute segment.

At the end of the segment, Kordich told viewers that he would send them free recipes if they would send a self-addressed stamped envelope to our office in Seattle. They posted our address at the end of the segment, for about 30 seconds.

The show with Kordich aired on June 30, right before the Fourth of July holiday weekend. Monday morning, my sister and I are sitting in the office in Seattle when the mail truck pulls up out front. The mailman gets out of the truck carrying a large canvas mail sack over his shoulder, which he brings into our office and says: "This is for you." He goes back outside two more times and returns with mail sacks stuffed with letters.

That single appearance generated more than 15,000 letters requesting free juice recipes! We knew Kordich was good, but we were overwhelmed. My sister and I went down to the local printer and produced a one-page sheet of juice recipes plus a one-page sales brochure for the juice machine. We spent the rest of the week answering every letter—by hand. That one event helped us sell more than a hundred juice machines, generating over $30,000 in sales. We were on our way!

Everything I had learned up to that point went into the development of our long-term strategy for the Juiceman. Our short-term strategy was very simple: to book Kordich on as many talk shows as we could, using the "free recipe" response idea to generate as much interest as possible. But our bigger goal was: How can we create a *long-term* business with this product, and build a brand?

At the time (late 1980s and early 1990s), plenty of direct response television campaigns were expanding into new product categories. The number of cosmetics, fitness equipment, and kitchenware products sold via DRTV were growing. Many of these companies quickly discovered, much to their detriment, that there were no service providers equipped to handle the back-end, behind-the-scenes aspects of the infomercial sale. Support systems we take for granted today—such as a call center for phone answering, automated billing services, and order fulfillment—were still in their infancy.

In those days, direct response television was a mostly temporary front-end-driven business, focused on immediate response. Few entrepreneurs back then showed any interest in developing lifetime clients by offering value and service. The whole field was still fairly opportunistic, and not much interested in providing excellent customer service. No one was thinking in terms of long-term consumer relationships.

Most companies would develop and sell a product until it peaked and then simply move on, leaving all the hard work they had invested behind. The idea that DRTV could be aimed at developing ongoing relationships that would add value and sell additional product was beyond conception. Looking at this industry during this period, versus who's still in operation today, it becomes apparent that the companies that survived are those that were really willing and able to focus on taking care of their customers.

We weren't interested in a flash-in-the-pan explosion that would burn out quickly and be unsustainable. The first task was to get Kordich on local radio and television talk shows in specific local markets. We accomplished this through fairly standard public relations methods. We were introduced by a producer on the *Richard Bey Show* to a couple of young guys who were just getting started in the business: Eric Yaverbaum and John Sawyer. Their company was called Jericho Communications. They turned out to be geniuses at PR and the perfect fit for what we were trying to do. I still work with Eric to this day; he is also the author of several books, including the popular *Public Relations For Dummies*.

Live Seminars

The system worked like this in those days: The two of us would arrive in a city, whenever and wherever Kordich was scheduled by our publicist to appear for an interview on radio and/or television. During the interview he announced our free seminar. It didn't matter whether it was a local talk show, morning program, or any combination of these. At the end of his appearance, Kordich announced that he was offering a free lecture, in whatever conference room or rooms we'd reserved in the area, to explain more about juicing.

At these seminars Kordich offered a lot of thought-provoking and useful information about the health benefits of fresh juice. Then came the demonstration portion, when he put the product through its paces, live-action. Of course, when people arrived to hear the free lecture and see the demonstration, we always had plenty of juice machines on hand for sale after the presentation. We used this approach for about a year, with moderate success.

For the time being, we stuck to our normal public relations/lecture format that was the cornerstone of our business. But in the background our direct response show was in the works. Even when he was at home Kordich would do radio interviews with stations all over the country. These, of course, were still being booked by our public relations firm. At the end of each radio interview, or "segment," he gave out a 1-800 phone number that people could call for more information. We followed up with a brochure that offered more detailed information about the juicer; these we sent to callers through the mail.

This is the second most important result of the odd way things developed for us: the customer contact information we gathered—practically without cost or effort. Our first database was an "accidental" collection of contact information for 15,000 health-conscious consumers. To that we added our barnstorming customers, and it grew and grew. Every time Kordich was interviewed or appeared on some morning show, no matter how obscure or small the market, we gathered more names for our database. This influx generated huge business.

The public relations fees we shelled out for booking these appearances and interviews were nominal compared to the benefits, which proved to be tremendous. At the time, our response rates for these public relations appearances were comparable to the standard response rates for direct response infomercials on radio or television, *minus* the advertising cost. So for us in the early days, the appearances and the follow-up letters and calls were the foundation that supported the growth of our company. This feedback ended up being an important element of the business.

Plus, back then, public relations appearances offered much higher "credibility" than any other form of advertising. In the early days of the business, all we did was move around from city to city, doing appearances, giving lectures, and selling product after the seminars. People would show up at the lectures and we'd sell them the product. Or people would call one of the 1-800 numbers and request more information or make purchases.

In the beginning, marketing the Juiceman seemed to inevitably run ahead of manufacturing. We were never really able to cut loose and open the throttle to experiment with the marketing ventures we'd conceived of because we were constantly playing catch-up with the manufacturing.

Eventually, Kordich sat down with the engineers of Thielmann-Rotel Know-How AG, manufacturers in Switzerland. He explained all the features he wanted for the juicer. Together, he and Rotel developed a juicer that was still head and shoulders above market competitors at the time. Early on, I flew to the Rotel plant in Poland, to coordinate our marketing plan with the factory and make our manufacturing requirements very clear.

Ultimately, we ended up hiring an American engineering firm to update the juice machine. We literally shopped the globe to find the best manufacturing relationship we could, one that would allow us to really get the product into the public consciousness. Eventually, we settled on a Korean manufacturing company that did a lot of private-label manufacturing for other reputable companies, like Samsung.

One of the biggest reasons I got involved with the Juiceman was Jay Kordich's fantastic presence. Almost from the beginning it was evident that *he* was a real draw, not just the product. Despite this, we held off making our first infomercial for almost two years. I had all the necessary knowledge to go out and make one right away, but the last thing I wanted was to roll out an effective infomercial and not be able to keep up with manufacturing. It was a simple supply-and-demand problem. The fact that manufacturing capabilities in Poland wouldn't have been able to keep up was one of the reasons we waited two years before hitting television with a 1-800 number.

There was another reason for holding back until we were absolutely sure we were prepared. I had enough experience to realize that as soon as we hit the television market with our 1-800 sales number, competitors would start to crawl out of the wood-work. I knew we had a small window of opportunity to be the only game in town once the direct response show went on air. Before long competitors would tap into the product and the show, to exploit our solid market base. I was afraid that once we hit the small screen, the product's life cycle would be rela-tively short. That was something we absolutely didn't want to happen.

All along Kordich and I were careful to ensure that every-thing we did contributed to our overall long-term plan to build a strong sustainable business foundation. We knew that once we launched the infomercial on a big scale, we had to be poised to shift into retail, at lightning speed, to stay a step ahead of the knockoffs. Although there were some bumps and turns along the way, things eventually worked out as planned.

It was kind of a no-brainer to realize that the response would be big. After all, a *single* 20-minute TV appearance with Richard Bey had resulted in more than 15,000 letters.

CHAPTER
5

Building the Juiceman® Brand

There are a lot of seemingly small decisions that go into developing a successful DRTV campaign designed to build a brand. Because we knew that Jay Kordich was our spokesperson, the things we had to decide were more geared to the style and format.

When we started planning, a potential idea struck me. Kordich had been really successful on Richard Bey's television show. They had a great rapport and Bey was a recognizable television professional. I thought, "Why don't we just call Richard Bey and see if he'll fly to Seattle to host the infomercial." Much to our relief, he was interested. At the time I was working with a successful television producer named Dan Riley. Dan was and still is a hard "Juicer," and he helped me recreate the format that had been so successful on the *Richard Bey Show*.

Because Kordich had so many years experience, we didn't really have to do much to craft a script. The plan was to let him and Bey interact naturally in front of a live studio audience, just as if it were a "regular" talk show. We'd decided the television show would use the direct response format because feedback had been so positive. We supplied Bey with a clear outline of the important discussion points. These were based on the kinds of questions that we found in the initial letters, supplemented by two years' worth of PR appearances and live seminars. I just highlighted target topics that I wanted Bey to prompt Kordich to talk about. The call-to-action of the show pitched the free nationwide seminars, where attendees could learn more about the product and purchase a juicer. Take note that, at the outset, the infomercials promoted the live seminars.

Initially, we shot three half-hour shows, then edited the best pieces together. The entire show, including compensation for Richard Bey, cost less than $40,000. But that was in 1991. Today, the half-hour infomercials we produce can cost from $300 to over $500 thousand.

The first Juiceman infomercial was made in the spring of 1991. The show not only demonstrated the Juiceman Juicer but educated viewers on the health benefits of fresh juicing. Since we'd always had a positive response in Salt Lake City, where the people tended to be health conscious, we first tested the show there. Ordinarily, when buying infomercial time, you purchase an allotment of times grouped together. Over a weekend, for instance, I'd buy Saturday afternoon through Tuesday, spending anywhere from $15,000 to $100,000, depending on the size of the city. In Salt Lake City, I know I spent somewhere between $15,000 and $18,000 for airtime, and booked several hotel conference rooms for the follow-up seminars. In our experience until that point, promoting seminars through the standard public relations method, we usually drew between 100 to 400 people to the live seminar in any given city.

For me, this is the most exciting part of the infomercial process: when you've finished the show and you get to put it to the test. It doesn't matter if it's a seminar show or an infomercial, you sit there holding your breath, your fingers crossed, waiting for the results. During our Salt Lake City test, more than 600 people showed up at the first hotel location, and we still had two more days for the show to run. That indicated to us right away that the infomercial would be a phenomenal success.

Over the course of the next year, we hired speakers, usually professionals in the health and nutrition field—naturopathic doctors, nutritionists, even some MDs—to give Kordich's health lecture. The seminars helped promote the business in several ways. We sent speakers, including Kordich, into the target city. While the seminars were ongoing we also booked local public relations appearances, all while simultaneously running the infomercials. We were killing three birds with one stone.

By combining all three types of media, we benefited exponen-tially from the buzz we generated. We were using multi-media marketing before the term was invented!

Explosive Growth

When we started our public relations touring in 1989, the total number of juicers sold at retail hovered just under 300,000 a year. Few retailers had them in stock, and apparently no one had the capacity to manufacture juicers quickly. As a result of our success, however, trade papers started taking notice and juicers started selling like hotcakes in retail stores. We must have made companies that had juicers for sale at the time a ton of money. Juicers of all makes and models began flying off the shelves. This is one of the powerful aspects of direct response that many people still do not understand, but that has been the basis for almost all of the successful projects I have done: that is, the ability to drive product through retail channels. A lot of people with large companies, which market products for a living, still do not understand this concept, even though it has been proven over and over again, with Juiceman, the George Foreman Grill, Sonicare, OxiClean, and many more. Even with all this evidence, these people seem to think that it will not work for "my product"; but it will, if you just give it a chance.

In August of 1991, when our long-form television show debuted with a 1-800 number, in concert with the outreach created by our seminars, everything was working great. In 1989, we did $.5 million in sales; in 1990, $6 million; in 1991, $30 million; and in 1992, almost $75 million in annual sales. Suddenly, the Juiceman was no longer a small business. People were starting to write about it, hear about it, and, more impor-tantly, buy it!

The television show worked great for promoting the semi-nars, as well. In a city like Los Angeles, we'd schedule lectures at five different locations over the course of a week. We spread the appearances all over, from venues in Santa Monica to Pasadena. At times we even organized two lectures a day. Altogether, we sold almost 2,000 units over the course of a single week in Los Angeles. That's about $500,000 in revenue for doing only one week of seminars.

The juicer trend hit so big and so fast it created huge demand, causing many companies that were not in it before to jump into the juicer business. The top of the market was impossible to predict. As the wave of interest in, and consumer demand for, juicers was growing, no one knew that everyone else was scrambling behind the scenes to fill that growing demand by manufacturing. Eventually, it became clear that the juicer market peaked somewhere between 2 and 3 million units, the level of annual sales we reached our third year on the air. It was about the same time that a glut of other manufacturers' juicers hit the market.

Retail Strategy

Switching a successful direct response campaign to retail can be a tricky proposition. Sustaining both distribution avenues is a precarious balancing act.

The key for us was to devise a strategy that allowed the infomercial to stimulate retail sales while simultaneously keeping the retail sales from affecting the direct response business. That's a big challenge. We resolved this using a new approach: We sold two entirely different units. Today this is fairly standard practice, but in the early to mid-1990s it was a breakthrough. Remember, big-box warehouse outlets like Sam's Club and Walmart were just emerging at the time. Now it's not uncommon to find each distributor selling a product model unique to its market and price point; for us, then, it was an innovative solution.

In the beginning, the Juiceman (the second revised version of the product we had developed) was the infomercial product. The standard Juiceman could *only* be bought through 1-800 numbers broadcast during the television spots or at the seminars. The Juiceman Jr., on the other hand, was specially designed and introduced to serve a slightly lower price point.

Our reason for developing a less expensive version of the product was to compete with similar products by other manufacturers that were experiencing retail success, basically by riding on our coattails. We rolled out to retail in a very slow and controlled manner. At first, the only outlets were health food stores, because they served our core consumer. Later we introduced the Juiceman Jr to department stores.

Then, because our high-end, or infomercial, product was truly better, stronger, and faster, and was therefore better adapted to the specific demands of health juicing, we released the Juiceman into the health food stores. These initial retail sales had little to no effect on the infomercial sales, in part because the health food store price was the same as the television price. But as we went forward in the process, it was the retail outlets that pushed the product prices lower and lower.

A strategy I still use today is to sell the most expensive unit or package on TV and put out a less expensive unit in retail. The consumer pays more for the TV product but usually receives a larger package of products. For example, customers who bought the Juiceman on TV received a package of books and tapes about juicing, not available at retail.

Due to the huge market demand for the Juiceman, I was a little less conservative than I usually am. The trade papers kept reporting that stores all over the country were selling out of other manufacturers' juicers, so I was in a hurry to get our product into retail.

To make my job slightly less complicated, we opted to work with the largest national distributor of small appliances in the country, Professional Housewares Distributors, Inc., which handled rival products like Black & Decker, Oster, and others. Professional Housewares Distributors, Inc., made it possible for us to get our product into stores nationwide incredibly fast, compared to what we might have accomplished alone. But by going through a distributor, we lost touch with the kind of direct feedback that had enabled me to keep my finger on the pulse of our business from the very beginning. Using a distributor interrupted that important link. We no longer had access to detailed information about how many units were actually being sold at retail. We could, of course, see the distribution reports, but I lost contact with the actual number of sales that were being made in the retail outlets.

We opted to work with an experienced distributor simply because we had the manufacturing capability. We had access to products that other manufacturers simply couldn't keep on the shelves. Our retail distributor urged us to go national in the first few months. The result? We went from zero retail business to retail sales as high as 80 percent of our business in less than a year. For us, going national happened like a shot. It seemed that almost overnight our product was everywhere at once.

That said, if I had to do it over, I would have dealt with a couple of retailers, mastered the learning curve, and figured out how the retail business works. To stay in line with our long-term strategy, going directly to the retailers on a much smaller basis initially would have made more sense. It's better to slowly spread product out to all appropriate retailers than it is to try and cover the map in one fell swoop.

Kordich had an uncanny ability to get people excited about juicing, it's true. But the Juiceman product's longevity was also due in part to the scientific or educational perspective of the infomercials. We used our advertising to build a national brand, one that is still going strong in stores today. We did this by taking the long-term view. We did not cut any corners. We established a scientific advisory board, offered the best nutritional support information, and published books on juicing. Jay Kordich's *Juiceman's Power of Juicing* became number one on the *New York Times* How-to Best Sellers list, with more than 500,000 copies sold. We published another book called *Juicing for Life: A Guide to the Benefits of Fresh Fruit and Vegetable Juicing,* which has sold more than 750,000 copies.

Hundreds of professional athletes started drinking freshly extracted juices to improve their performance—the entire Texas Rangers team, several of the Los Angeles Dodgers, even some of the Milwaukee Brewers. Nolan Ryan called the office one day and ordered a juicer. Mark McGuire did an unpaid testimonial for us. Carl Lewis bought several juicers, and went so far as to credit drinking fresh juices with helping him maintain a high performance level. We had lots of showbiz celebrities, as well, order our juicers. It was always a kick for our in-house phone operators to get a call from a celebrity ordering a juicer; among them were Bill Murray, Kirstie Alley, Randy Travis, Bruce Willis, and Demi Moore.

I began to realize that the DRTV model I used with the Juiceman Juicer could be applied to other products. It could be used not just to increase sales but to build brands, as well. To build a powerful brand in a DRTV campaign requires establishing an emotional connection with the consumer, to inspire a deep, long-lasting relationship. This is the kind of brand identification the Juiceman created. Our clearly defined health and nutrition position helped consumers identify with our brand. People understood the benefits of our company brand and wanted to be associated with it.

One of the factors too many don't take into consideration is that brand connection doesn't end with the tone and quality of the TV spot. The "brand persona" must be recognizable at each and every single point of contact between the consumer and the company. This includes all media, print, radio, television, or Internet; the packaging; and, most especially, customer service and order fulfillment.

The emotional connection to and interest in the product generated by the DRTV show can all too easily be diluted or destroyed by poorly trained or rude call center operators or by an annoying shopping cart glitch on a web site. The brand relationship is about trust. Customers trust that the brand will deliver, and perhaps exceed expectations in all areas. This includes the product, market positioning, and every facet of customer service.

CHAPTER
6

Expanding the Brand

The Breadman®

One of the biggest advantages of building our company through seminars the way we did with the Juiceman was the extensive customer database we accumulated over time. Because we grew pretty much in a grassroots fashion, we attracted consumers who were passionate about health and nutrition; people who were ideologically aligned with our company's goals. After all, it takes a lot to motivate a potential customer to get up off the couch to attend a seminar (even if it's free) just to find out more about juicing.

The people in our database ended up being a gold mine of information and recurring sales. For instance, when our engineering department developed a new juicer blade-basket combo that delivered 20 percent more juice, we sent out a simple postcard (this was before e-mail marketing existed) to our database, and it generated over $500,000 in sales. We also explored ideas for potential new products after the Juiceman through surveys mailed to our database customers.

We found that our customers had a growing interest in eating healthier, and were looking for easier ways to do it. Juicing was an easy way to get more fruits and vegetables in their diets. We decided we could do the same thing for whole grains, with a bread machine. Hence, the Breadman was born.

Few people knew much about bread-making machines, and didn't know how to evaluate which one to buy. It was the Juiceman machine's top-brand-name quality that led customers to feel they could depend on our company for quality and reliability. They were more than willing to turn to us for more quality products as a result of their positive experiences with the Juiceman.

Customer relations are, and have been, one of the most important aspects of a successful strategy for building a brand.

Customer service was our highest priority. Some companies in our field came into the business with a mind-set to make a lot of money as quickly as possible, sell a lot of product in the short term, and not care what happens to the customer down the road. When sales slow down, they drop the product and move on to the next one. This type of short-term thinking has hurt the direct response business over the years and given it a bad reputation.

Our careful cultivation of consumer respect made it possible for us to reap long-term benefits. As a result of the way we treated our customers, people were willing to come back to us again and again. The high quality of the Juiceman machines, of the infomercials, plus our customer follow-through, helped consumers establish a sense of trust in our company. They *knew* the company not only offered quality products, but that we stood behind them, as well.

We decided to develop a bread-making machine not because it was a bull's-eye infomercial product, but because health and nutrition were the crux of our company's mission; and our market research revealed it was something our consumers were interested in. This kind of product was definitely in alignment with our overall mission of making healthier eating easier and more accessible for everyone. Sure, everyone knows that eating more fruits and vegetables, more whole grains, and legumes is a healthier choice. But few of us have the time, money, and focus it takes to do a complete overhaul of our pantries, our day-to-day habits, and regular ways of doing things to make these healthy changes.

The juicer was one incredibly efficient way to help people make that transition. The Juiceman made it much easier for people to get more fruits and vegetables in their diets. Therefore, helping people get more whole grains into their daily diets was a logical next step. So from a health and nutrition point of view, the bread-making machine was a great next product for our company to offer our target consumer.

Because there wasn't a comfortable profit margin with the bread maker, most companies wouldn't have gone the infomercial route. Evaluating the bread machine solely in terms of economic viability, the "right" profit margins just weren't there in terms of an infomercial product.

We chose to look at the Breadman bread machine in terms of the company's mission. By factoring in the idea that we were establishing ourselves in the retail market as purveyor of products that make it easier for people to eat and live healthy, it became a simple choice. The company was also acutely aware that, thanks to our strong consumer following, the Breadman was the kind of product that could ride into retail on the Juiceman's coattails. Even though it would have only average earnings from the infomercial approach, there was much more that went into the decision to develop the Breadman.

Validating "the Model"

If Trillium had been just an infomercial company looking for a product, we wouldn't have chosen the bread maker. That's one of the reasons similar products haven't popped up on television since then. We wanted to use all the systems and ideas we mastered while creating the Juiceman. After finding a manufacturer and a product that was efficient and reliable, it was time to start thinking about the infomercial. After giving it a lot of thought, I homed in on a spokesperson named George Burnett.

Burnett was originally brought in as one of the seminar speakers for the Juiceman, after we had diversified and the seminars were no longer all put on by Jay Kordich. So it was clear to me that Burnett could work a crowd and sell a product. It just so happened that Burnett and his family had owned and operated a natural foods bakery in Montana for 20 years. Burnett was also a natural-food lecturer and baker who was successfully spreading the word about the important benefits of whole-grain natural breads.

Rather than co-opting a known personality I decided to take a different, more interesting approach by creating a "Breadman" personality. Burnett was a good choice for the role, based on his history and experience. We followed all the steps we learned during the Juiceman experience but compressed the whole process into a shorter time frame. We put the product into retail, started our publicity tour, and released the book all on the same day the infomercial premiered.

We organized a 35-city public relations tour that would be going on simultaneously with all the other releases and openings. Everything put in place for the Breadman rollout went down over a very short three-month period. We planned it that way intentionally, to take advantage of the retail sales from the minute the television show hit the air. Although we did use a book in the Juiceman rollout, it didn't come until much later in the process.

Burnett's bread book, on the other hand, worked really well to help promote both him and the product. Until *The Breadman's Healthy Bread Book* hit the market, most bread machine recipes were full of white flour, refined white sugar, saturated fats, and artificial flavors. Burnett's recipes were much different. A full 70 percent used absolutely no white flour, instead replacing it with highly nutritious multigrains—or, at the very least, unbleached flour.

The Breadman's book offered simple recipes for delicious whole-grain breads that were sweetened *without sugar*, had almost no saturated fats, and were low in calories. All of the recipes used minimal amounts of honey and/or molasses as sweetener. These breads contained no refined sugar at all, and no shortening either. Perhaps most importantly, all the recipes worked well in the Breadman-brand bread machines.

My favorite part of the book, though, was where Burnett described his healthful lifestyle philosophy. He took the time to explain that the different parts of a wheat kernel and other types of grains and legumes are more healthful for bread. His book really promoted the benefits of making healthy lifestyle changes by using the bread machine. He demonstrated that it was possible to make healthful loaves of bread that promoted, rather than inhibited, weight loss and lower cholesterol, and introduced vitamins, minerals, and fiber into the diet naturally.

These were the kinds of benefits we highlighted during the long-form show that aired on television. But when the infomercial didn't work as well as we'd hoped, we went back to the drawing board and made a few changes that really increased its effectiveness. The retail sales were solid right from the get-go. It also helped that *Consumer Reports* named the Breadman the best bread machine on the market. After the report came out, we couldn't keep the machines in stock, and had to fly in containers to meet consumer demand.

By sticking to our company mission, we were able to develop an unusual follow-up product that sold well, especially among our existing customer database. Even though the Breadman product lacked the kind of profit margin an infomercial product should usually demonstrate to be successful, we managed a moderate success in the short course of three months. What took us three or more years to accomplish with the Juiceman we compressed into three months, to make the Breadman concept profitable enough to be worthwhile.

Selling the Business

By the end of 1992, our business had become mostly retail in nature, but my heart and soul was still in direct-to-consumer marketing. When our long-term success attracted the attention of a large company by the name of Salton, based in Chicago, we decided to sell Trillium and both product lines to Salton, based on its tremendous sales record. As retail distribution expanded, sales skyrocketed to $100 million. The Juiceman Juicer solidified itself as the first major national brand created by a DRTV campaign. We had completed the cycle and crossed the finish line, winners. I took a few months off.

When Salton took over the Juiceman and began its own series of infomercials the company discovered that even if infomercial sales only broke even, retail sales would skyrocket. Salton became big believers in the infomercial/retail marketing model. Soon after, it would launch the largest-selling infomercial product of all time, the George Foreman Grill.

Sonicare®

The $150 Toothbrush

After the sale of the Trillium Company in 1993, I slowed down for a bit. I developed a shell company called Cesari Direct and just let it sit while I learned to breathe again. Over the past five years I had built two products under the banner of a single brand that were successful enough to be scooped up by Salton, Inc. I ran a business that had up to 180 employees at one time. After the sale I was simply enjoying life in Seattle and didn't have any concrete plans.

Then a former business partner by the name of Bob Lamson gave me a ring at home. He told me there was a start-up company in Bellevue that was looking to do the same type of marketing we had done for the Juiceman. The company was called Optiva Corporation, and was a one-product business at the time. The challenge was that Optiva was having tremendous difficulty getting its product into retail distribution. The big roadblock that was making retailers resistant to its product was the price.

Optiva's product was a $150 toothbrush called Sonicare. Consumers in those days were used to paying between $5 and $7 for the most expensive toothbrushes on the market. There were a few electric toothbrushes on the market that were a bit more expensive, but even top-of-the-line models rarely crossed the $75 price mark, and Optiva's product was selling for twice that. What was different about this product that made it worth $150?

Although David Guliani, the CEO, and Eric Meyer, the director of marketing at Optiva, were excellent businessmen, their product faced an immense challenge getting into retail outlets and attracting consumers. They needed a way to convince people, retailers, and consumers alike that shelling out

$150 on a toothbrush had a long-term value. It took incredible foresight for these two businessmen to take a risk on an infomercial in 1994. Well into the 1990s, infomercials were considered suspect, or somehow "less than" regular brand advertising. It was a common perception then that using an infomercial would ultimately hurt the brand. Meyer admits outright, "I was frankly a bit concerned about how a DR campaign would impact the young Sonicare brand. Even though we created a premium production, I was still a bit worried about guilt by association with Ginsu knives." Clearly, the stigma against direct response television still existed at the time of the Sonicare toothbrush show.

But the management at Optiva had an excellent background in manufacturing and brand building. They came to the conclusion that they could adapt these branding skills to the infomercial format. In truth, the Sonicare toothbrush is a product that was absolutely ideal for an infomercial. The extended duration of a long-form infomercial gave viewers enough time to learn and understand the benefits of the product well enough to override their initial resistance to the high price. A 30-minute infomercial is better for introducing a product that requires longer explanation and demonstration.

Problem/Solution

The Sonicare toothbrush provided us with the perfect opportunity to create the ultimate problem/solution show. Now, when it comes down to the nitty-gritty, all infomercials—actually, all commercials, even all advertising—boil down to a problem/solution message. Pitchmen in the expo buildings of state fairs across the country present products in a way that demonstrates how they can solve a problem the consumer is facing. The ones that catch your attention do so because you're familiar with that particular problem.

Brand advertisers do the same thing. How can you get stubborn stains like red wine and blood out of clothes? By using the right laundry detergent. How can you get that factory shine on your car? The right auto wax. Even retail stores can use the problem/solution setup. Where can you find the biggest selection at the lowest prices, thus saving both time and money? The right retail store. Talking about a problem in this way has the power to get people to take proactive steps that other approaches just can't match. The problem/solution message is absolutely necessary for a successful direct marketing approach.

The problem in this case was gum disease, and Sonicare was the solution. Our first goal was to educate consumers about gum disease. In those days, gum disease, though prevalent, was rarely discussed outside the dentist's office, and usually only when it was already a problem. Those conversations in the dentist's office were often the first time a person was even hearing of gum disease and dealing with the consequences.

We created a presentation that informed and educated people about what gum disease meant to them individually. All we had to do was explain how gum disease developed and then show them how the Sonicare toothbrush was a solution for that problem. Sonicare had a very strong unique selling proposition, or USP. It used sonic technology to clean beyond the reach of its bristles, to get to plaque bacteria in the nooks and crannies of your teeth, where other toothbrushes couldn't go. Hence, the famous tagline "Sonicare: Cleans beyond the bristles." This was actually the name of the infomercial we created for Optiva.

Our show demonstrated how the Sonicare toothbrush used new technology to kill the bacteria that causes gum disease. The management at Optiva had been active in educating and reaching out to the professional dental community about its product. It is very important when launching a new product like Sonicare to get the key opinion leaders in the field to endorse your product. Once you have the endorsement of the professional community, consumer sales will follow.

As part of the show's development, we took a film crew down to one of the biggest national dental trade shows, at the Moscone Center in San Francisco.

Credibility: The Key to a Successful Infomercial

At the San Francisco dental show we were able to talk with countless high-ranking experts in the field, among them deans of some of the most prestigious dental schools in the country. These are people that we in the industry refer to as *key opinion leaders*. One after another, these key opinion leaders stepped in front of the camera to extol the benefits of the Sonicare toothbrush. When you have the head of the Harvard School of Dental Medicine saying that your product is superior to others, it helps break down consumer skepticism, leading to a sale.

Since our goals for the show were to educate the consumer and develop strong credibility for the product, this approach was a tremendous asset to the broadcast. The other half of the equation was educating the consumer about how gum disease develops, the costs of gum disease, how prevalent it was despite the lack of public discourse on the problem. It didn't hurt to add that the treatment for many diagnoses of gum disease could be both costly and painful. It was then very easy to show how Sonicare could solve these problems for a lower cost, thereby creating a value proposition that people understood.

As I mentioned earlier in the book, another way to establish credibility is choosing the right host. I aimed for a highly respected, credible host for the Sonicare show. American actor Richard Dysart had a long track record of playing good-hearted physicians and kindly uncles; and twice he portrayed President Harry S. Truman. He is perhaps best known for his role as Leland McKenzie on the NBC legal drama *L.A. Law*, for which he earned one Emmy award and three more nominations as the head of the law firm. People tend to attribute the same characteristics to an actor as the role he or she is known for on TV, so Dysart was perfect to host our documentary-style show.

To back up our tremendous selection of expert testimonials, we had the kind yet serious Dysart moderating the show. We presented details of the clinical trials that proved Sonicare not only had reversed the effects of early-stage gum disease but that it also successfully whitened teeth. We used attractive graphics to demonstrate the dynamics of how the toothbrush actually worked. Once the show was developed and put together, we ran our first media test.

I was fortunate to do an entrepreneurial deal on this project. Initially, Optiva and I had put up the same amount of money to get the show made and on the air. It was organized in a way that my company would then earn royalties from sales. When we started, Optiva had annual sales in the range of less than $5 million. Two and a half years later, its sales topped $100 million!

When the show was at last complete, it was time to run our media tests. Media tests are the initial airings of the shows to determine whether the show will be successful or needs further tweaking or changes to be more effective.

We always media-test our edited infomercials in broadcast slots that have previously demonstrated excellent results. The reason being is you want to assess how well the TV shows will convert ad dollars into revenue. You also want to eliminate the variable if the show doesn't work: Was it the media time or the show that did not work? By putting it in tried-and-true media, we eliminate that variable.

We run the show for two consecutive weekends on our target media. This doubling up mitigates the effects of any news spikes that may distract viewers from their regular viewing habits. Something like the start of the Gulf War or a natural disaster that draws the focus of people all around the world and disrupts normal activity would adversely affect that weekend's test results. Hence, we schedule two consecutive media-test weekends to gather more accurate results.

The tool for determining the degree of success a show demonstrates is called the *media efficiency ratio*, or MER. It is the ratio of sales divided by the advertising cost. For example, if you generate $20,000 in sales from a $10,000 airtime buy, the MER is 2. The MER number provides a snapshot of an infomercial's success or failure.

The MER for the Sonicare's media tests were above 3:1. Three dollars earned for every dollar spent, which is an excellent ratio. This meant that our show was not only working but was going to be very successful. It was, in fact, educating *and* motivating viewers strongly enough to overcome the high price point, which is something a conventional advertising 30-second spot never could have managed.

Rolling Out a Campaign

Based on the results of the media test, we make decisions on how many advertising dollars to invest on a monthly basis. Optiva was an extremely well-run small company. It had achieved the triple crown of direct advertising. This is when a small company manages to get all three of the most important aspects of its business operating dynamically. It (1) offers an excellent product, (2) develops highly successful direct advertising for that product, and (3) has smart businesspeople at the helm to manage fast growth correctly. Companies like this can convert that initial blush of success into building brand equity and corporate value over the long term. Optiva Corporation eventually negotiated a very successful sale to Philips (it's now called Philips Oral Healthcare, Inc.). The other company we worked with that had all these attributes was Orange Glo International, (the makers of OxiClean), and not surprisingly, had a very profitable exit as well.

The direct response approach is an excellent choice for small businesses that want to launch a new product or service. The biggest benefit of DR is that it creates a subsidized advertising campaign. For a comparatively small advertising investment, these businesses can successfully earn income they can immediately reinvest in more and more advertising. In the Sonicare case, because of the revenue generated from direct sales the first year the infomercial rolled out, Optiva was able to spend over $6 million in national advertising. That enabled the company to quickly raise awareness and generate demand for its product.

The direct television campaign also becomes an engine that drives retail sales. This is why, at last, retailers are more than willing to carry infomercial products. They finally understand the powerful connection between television sales and pulling the product through retail distribution channels. As this process has evolved, a fairly reliable pattern has emerged, a pattern that we at Cesari Direct have identified and built into our branding and development process. In fact, despite his initial misgivings about the effects of direct response television on brand quality, Sonicare's Eric Meyer admits that, "Our DR efforts had no negative impact on brand. In fact, it built the formative stages of it."

It's not only experience that makes an expert. Continued success requires flexibility—the ability to respond to changes in the marketplace, in the economy, and in consumer buying patterns. Our model has been tried and tested and continues to evolve in response to each of the many products we launch annually.

The infomercial played an integral part in driving consumer awareness of the product. Sonicare's parent company, Optiva, experienced a 338 percent jump in sales between 1994 and 1996, meaning we did a lot of things right. Optiva took that success and then did a lot of things right as well, for which it was named *Inc.* magazine's number-one fastest-growing company and got talked up by Oprah—not just once, but three times!

Planning and sequencing distribution was disciplined. Early on, Costco courted Optiva. The membership warehouse chain wanted to carry Sonicare, but it was just too early in the process to put the product in retail. It hadn't even spread to the chain drugstores yet. Of course, Costco is a great retailer, and when the time was right it contributed to a huge percentage of total sales thanks to its modest margin requirements.

In retrospect, there were a few things we might have done differently to improve the results slightly or to gain even wider recognition across the market. Meyer, who was then Sonicare's vice president of marketing, has since pointed out that we might have been able to extend the Sonicare brand more broadly, from high end to low end. But at the time the products to cover those options weren't in development. This is something we learned from the infomercial's success.

Later, the Sonicare Elite did evolve and take over as the top-of-the-line product for the brand. When it was rolled out, the "old" Sonicare toothbrushes were shifted into a medium price range. So, eventually, we did cover those elements of the marketplace.

In the late 1990s, a low-end price category for this product was emerging, but Sonicare wasn't prepared to capitalize on it at the time. Other less expensive products, such as the Dr. John's SpinBrush (later acquired by P&G) did very well. Optiva didn't have the time or energy to take into full consideration that a lower-end spin brush market might emerge. So it's possible that there was a missed opportunity to welcome consumers at the low end of the price category, which had comparatively high-volume sales. On the other hand, such a move might have backfired and tainted the Sonicare premium brand recognition that we had established.

Sure, there were a lot of surprises to deal with, and lots of speed bumps. But every campaign has those. Rollouts are like marathons or mountain climbing—you can never give up!

The Biggest Knockout in History

George Foreman exuded an everyman quality. He somehow came across as an uncommon man with the common touch. Our creative staff was able to couple the engaging personality of this champion boxer with a clunky taco maker to capture the fancy of the public in a way that no one could have ever imagined. The proper message and a charming on-air posture delivered phenomenal profits for Foreman and Salton—plus one of the world's most recognized brands. The challenges were many, however, including how to endear this huge man—6 feet 3 inches and more than 250 pounds—to a mostly female audience. A major piece of the solution was to expose and maximize his charismatic smile, big heart, and established credibility, *and* reposition a curious, tilted taco machine.

How a Champion Boxer and a Failed Taco Maker Created Sizzling Success

In the mid-1990s, Salton Inc. experimented with several innovative kitchen appliances. Because of our long-standing, positive relationship with Salton, which began and prospered during our Juiceman years, we worked together often. Salton had seen time and again how targeted, creative campaigns stimulated big spikes in retail sales for household products— the kind of products Salton specializes in. The company's CEO, Leon Dreimann, first brought us a bagel maker. We did a test, but in the end we determined the bagel maker had too fine a profit margin for it to work as an infomercial product. The price point was high and consumers weren't highly motivated. Here's why:

It became clear immediately that purchasing bagels at the grocery store was less time-consuming and expensive for shoppers than making their own fresh bagels at home. In addition, there was some psychological resistance on the part of consumers to the idea of eliminating their comfortable daily routine of stopping at the corner diner for a coffee and bagel, or doughnut, or whatever, on their way to work. The bagel maker didn't really solve an urgent consumer "problem" and was therefore not an "urgent" purchase. These are some of the first questions entrepreneurs and new inventors need to ask themselves: Is my product solving a problem? Will I be able to instill a sense of urgency in a consumer's purchasing decision?

The next kitchen item that Salton sent our way was a taco maker. It was a contraption with a closing lid; it had some vague similarities to a waffle iron, but was rectangular, not square. It was deemed and configured to be a fast, convenient way to brown ground beef and other meats for taco filling. The tilted grilling surface was a simple design enhancement that made it easier to take out the browned ground beef, separated from its grease. The grill was presented at household industry trade shows to a largely uninterested public.

Salton looked for a spokesperson to introduce the grill. At the same time, a celebrity agent, attorney Sam Perlmutter, was on the lookout for product endorsement opportunities for his client, George Foreman, the two-time World Heavyweight Boxing Champion and Olympic gold medalist. The collaboration between Foreman and Salton began as an uncertain gamble that turned into a legendary gold mine—and 100 million grills sold.

Foreman, at this stage of his life, was not a hot pop star or an upstart athlete garnering big endorsement deals or movie cameos. In 1996, George Foreman wasn't even young anymore, but that didn't bother our company. We had worked with mature spokespeople on a variety of products and enjoyed some significant success. And although neither Mason Adams nor Richard Dysart, a couple of the older actors we had used as spokespersons, had the same kind of "celebrity," they did share some qualities with Foreman. One of the most obvious similarities was their age. At 47, Foreman was supposed to be past his athletic prime, but he had just reclaimed the Heavyweight Championship of the World two years earlier, exactly 20 years after he first wore the heavyweight crown. We felt he was very appealing, and he seemed comfortable carrying this late-champ aura. While older men did not turn out to be our main targeted group, we sensed there were a certain number of backyard grillers and barbecuers who identified with Foreman and knew he was the oldest man ever to become heavyweight champion. More importantly, he turned out to be a wonderful, down-to-earth guy with a huge heart and great sense of humor. He did not travel with a large, loud entourage like other high-profile champions, athletes, or musicians. He had one man, who was his assistant, valet, bodyguard, and confidant. That was it.

The best spokesperson for a product is one who has used the product and genuinely believes that consumers can benefit by using it, too. The magic is getting the spokesperson to convey the "believability" to an audience, be it online, on television or radio, or in print. We were privileged to be a part of several campaigns with terrific spokespersons who believed in what they were selling, including one who featured one of the top-grossing products of all time.

George Foreman's pleasure in food was well established. Since 1989, when he launched his comeback into the boxing ring, he had become the spokesperson for many companies, including McDonald's. When he became the oldest boxer to win the heavyweight title, he admitted that his training table meals consisted mainly of hamburgers. The idea that this former heavyweight champion boxer might be getting to "that" stage in life when it became important to get interested in healthy cooking made him credible on the subject. Add to that all his other qualities—father, preacher, president, and CEO of his own nonprofit youth organization. . . . He had another quality, as well, one found to be attractive to the American consumer: He was a southerner. Foreman was born in Marshall, Texas, deep in the heart of traditional grilling country.

The reason George Foreman was so perfect for the grill was that viewers coupled his status, age, and desire to eat better with the healthy lifestyle benefits of the grill. The clincher was his now-famous line at the end of every segment. He would make a fist and throw a short, right-cross punch, and say, "It knocks out the fat!" That became his signature line and motion.

Foreman became the brand because the connection between the grill and him was plausible. He surpassed his own celebrity status as a boxer to become the believable, guy-next-door, cooking a satisfying healthy meal on a Lean Mean Fat-Reducing Grilling Machine.

Successful celebrity branding transfers the value of the person to the product he or she endorses. Because Foreman was considered a solid citizen who was known to enjoy his food, and packed a punch of personality, he made a perfect spokesperson for a kitchen "must-have." His age and past experience as a finely tuned athlete helped to make him ideal to endorse the special innovations of Salton's fat-reducing grill.

After the first test, we discovered that between 60 and 70 percent of our target audience were females who lived in households earning $55,000 a year and were college educated. Not exactly the crowd known to take an interest in boxing. By simply removing the boxing footage and letting Foreman be Foreman in front of a live audience, we received much better results. Even though the grill was both new and different, and was a truly useful product, we needed to let the world see that Foreman had a great personality that matched it. Later on, when he demonstrated the grill on QVC, we would get huge spikes in sales every time he took a bite of the hamburger on camera. So we made sure to build in many of those moments to our future infomercials.

Barb Westfield, the former Salton vice president for brand development (who was lured away in 2002 to become the senior vice president of consumer marketing for Wolfgang Puck Worldwide, Inc.), was responsible for rolling out dozens of hotplates, ice cream systems, espresso machines, juice squeezers, and bread makers. She supplied a wonderful story about the extent of coupling George Foreman with that grill.

"I had to meet George at the airport in Seattle," Westfield recalled. "It was 2001, and he was flying in from Houston. As we were walking through the airport, a high school baseball team—all young boys—saw George Foreman as we were passing them. Suddenly, all these young kids yelled out in unison: 'It's the Lean Mean Grilling Machine!'

"Clearly, there was a big age difference. George brought a big recognition factor across a wide age demographic. George could connect with young and old."

There's no doubt that the Salton and George Foreman collaboration has been studied closely by others hoping to achieve an ideal endorsement match. Brand strategists and ad execs search constantly to find celebrities or athletes who might actually use their brand products in their day-to-day life. Athletes can't just carry a tote with a logo on it in front of the cameras on game days. That kind of "endorsement" no longer works.

Westfield said the decision to use George Foreman to promote the grill did not take long to make. Leon Dreimann, Salton's chairman and chief executive officer, simply assembled his marketing minds, to gauge their interest. A consensus was reached very quickly.

"Leon got about four of us in a room and asked us what we thought about using this massive guy as the spokesperson for this grill," Westfield said. "We thought we should give it a whirl because the man had just done something that spoke to baby boomers and seniors. He had reclaimed his heavyweight title in his 40s. Because of it, he became loved and trusted. He became the image for people to say 'why not?' to taking on challenges later in their lives."

Westfield also revealed several significant, simultaneous events that really "moved the needle" for grill sales at retail stores and on television offerings. First, the TV shows deleted the footage of Foreman's boxing history, to focus on food and grilling burgers. That move was coupled with the release of Foreman's new grilling cookbook, which included his favorite recipes and techniques.

"I think what really contributed to the momentum was a review of the product in the *New York Times* on New Year's Eve," Westfield said. "All of those people who were going to take the plunge on their resolutions regarding eating were hit with a lot of information from different directions at the same time. It made a huge difference."

At our company, we've used this example to show new inventors, existing clients, and potential customers how a number of avenues can build a solid foundation they can use for years. The combination and timing of the various offerings and media was critical. The whole was clearly greater than the sum of its parts. For example, when we're asked if a good public relations company is really worth the investment, we tell them how well-placed newspaper and magazine stories have truly aided a product in the past. Good PR is an invaluable piece of any marketing campaign.

Despite all the positives, we struggled initially to find a way to puzzle together Foreman and the indoor grill in the best possible way. For a first try, we bought some old footage of him during his boxing heyday—images from his most famous fights, against his most famous opponents, and from his most celebrated victories. We aired this footage in the early portion of a 30-minute paid program to remind viewers exactly who George Foreman was.

 Filming at George's Place

Taping at George's house north of Houston was always very interesting. On one occasion, our crew arrived at 8:00 AM and got everything set up to shoot. We just needed George to come down and get into makeup. We waited and waited; finally, he came down in his bathrobe and walked into the kitchen. He reminded me of what a big grizzly bear probably looks like the first day out of hibernation. It took him a little while to warm up, but once he got going, he was great. He has the smile of a little boy, and when he turns on the charm, he is hard to resist. People really like him.

One of our challenges to shooting in his home was that George is a big bird lover. He has a huge aviary in his backyard, with every type of tropical bird imaginable. Well, when you're trying to record audio, and you have 50 tropical birds, like parrots, whooping it up, it can get very frustrating.

It really is true that George Foreman has five sons, and they all are named George. He introduced me to each one: "Rick, this is George"; "Rick, this is George". . . . Then I met his daughter; she is named Georgette. George claims he did this because if he ever loses his memory as a result of taking so many blows to his head in the ring, he will always remember his kids' names. We actually did a scene in one of the shows with all his kids helping to cook burgers. It was just one more thing people loved about George.

It "Knocks Out the Fat"

I knew George loved food, but I really believe that the first time George ever used the product was when he walked onto the set the first day of taping. Also, I don't think he had really cooked anything himself in a long time. He had a wife, trainer, and personal cook who did that for him. So when he got on the set, it was a little awkward trying to get him to make anything. We solved that by switching roles with his co-host, Nancy Nelson. Nancy was a petite little blonde who looked very small next to George, but she had a lot of on-air experience. So we had her do all the cooking; George's role was to taste everything and comment how good it was. It turned out that was the formula for success. It was proven then and later when George was on the QVC Channel. Every time he tasted the food, the sales calls would spike. We also created for him a now-famous line at the end of every segment. He would make a fist and throw a short, right-cross punch and say, "It knocks out the fat!" That became his signature line and motion.

We structured the 30-minute format to give viewers time enough to connect with Foreman. The shows contained much of the experience and lessons we learned and refined over time with the Juiceman and Sonicare. However, unlike those two products, which were sold live via 1-800 numbers and, ultimately, web incentives, we needed to build a campaign geared to selling the George Foreman Grill in retail stores. One of the most important factors of the product, and of the show, was that Foreman wasn't telling people they needed to go on a restrictive diet to eat healthy. He had a guy-next-door way of getting viewers involved in his real passion for food. Then he added the bonus of health benefits, which made the grill irresistible.

The Foreman Grill represented not just a "grill," but the personal image it created for buyers. People admired Foreman's physical prowess, his geniality. Therefore, they could imagine themselves "hanging out with him," wanting to be like him. All of this was the result of just letting him show viewers how easy it was to retain that vigor and energy—if they had the grill. The show associated having a firm, fit, albeit aging, body like Foreman's with having the grill. But it was his credible, positive image that packed an emotional, effective sales pitch. One of the unexpected bonuses of working with Foreman turned out to be his plausibility. The show depicted him having fun cooking with a fat-reducing grill. He was enjoying all his favorites, made better and healthier through the properties of the grill. If a heavyweight boxer can have fun doing it, then it's worth a try.

Marketing experts say Foreman's connection with consumers comes not from his achievements in the ring, but rather from his own remarkable personal transformation. A caustic, detached boxer in his early years became a happy, engaging entrepreneur when he relaunched his ring career in 1989. He became so believable as the guy behind the grill that people wrote him directly and sent e-mails. He was asked for his favorite recipes, and whether he had tips to properly maintain the grill. This emotional association and personal connection is crucial for building any brand and a loyal market.

In 1996, George Foreman was an unlikely icon. A well-managed celebrity endorsement changed all that. He was able to convey that just as he was benefiting from the unique "fat-knocking" quality of a grill's tilted surface, ordinary people could as well, simply by owning one.

The natural extension of all this is that the brand, when executed properly, actually surpasses the celebrity. Today, George Foreman is no longer remembered only as a two-time heavyweight boxing champion of the world and Olympic gold medalist, who won 76 of his 81 professional bouts, 68 of those by knocking out his opponent. George Foreman is more readily recognized in association with a brand and product: the George Foreman Lean Mean Fat-Reducing Grilling Machine.

The Price of Celebrity

At first glance, the George Foreman Grill has little to do with the tennis world. But not too long ago, the brand drafted former tennis champion Monica Seles to share her story of good eating habits and healthy living and endorse the George Foreman Grill. That's the power of establishing strong branding. How many products can you recall that continued to thrive without the presence of its namesake?

The Foreman-Salton marriage has proven to be an ideal example of what is possible when you combine celebrity endorsement with effective branding. Obviously, not all celebrity spokespeople work out as well as George Foreman. There are two key risks when a company considers aligning itself with a particular celebrity spokesperson or endorser.

- *Term of contract.* How long will this person maintain his or her popularity? This is especially true if the individual's celebrity is based on his or her performance, status, or ranking. The shelf life of any celebrity will vary as a result of trends, performance, and public perception. Jessica Simpson did wonders for Proactiv a few years ago, but her stardust has faded a bit since then. Being stuck with a long-term contract with her wouldn't be that great a benefit to a marketing firm at this point in time. This demonstrates the first major issue any inventor, creator, or entrepreneur needs to consider before aligning his or her product with an individual celebrity.

- *Potential liability.* Every celebrity is under the microscope, some more than others; just ask Brittany Spears. Their private lives, personal integrity, and public behavior are constantly judged and evaluated, sometimes on a minute-by-minute basis (thanks, Twitter). If your celebrity spokesperson is implicated in any kind of scandal, it could ruin the brand, or at least put a devastating dent in the product's public perception of it. We've all heard about these kinds of deals going south when the celebrity in question suddenly attracts the wrong kind of publicity. The biggest risk to the product *and* company is the celebrity him- or herself.

There's another way of thinking, that any publicity is good publicity. Some companies will try to manipulate the bad publicity of a celebrity to market a product, but this is a very delicate line to walk. Weight-loss program brand Jenny Craig lost public affection when it hired an overweight Monica Lewinsky to lose over 50 pounds for an alleged $1 million—a deal she did not fulfill.

Public opinion drives spokesperson decisions. TV commentator Bill O'Reilly spearheaded a successful write-in campaign to get PepsiCo to fire hip-hop sensation Ludacris because of his raunchy lyrics. The singer was let go from Pepsi's endorsement roster with the public announcement that he lacked the requirements to represent the mega-soda brand. Ozzy Osbourne then led a protest, claiming that Pepsi's ousting of Ludacris at the behest of a vocal minority was hypocritical. Pepsi was forced to put together a compromise instead. Although Pepsi has a history of successful celebrity endorsements, it occasionally faces a challenge that demonstrates how delicate the arrangement between celebrity and brand really is.

Sometimes a brand will contract an aspiring athlete or entertainer based on expectation of future success. Nike's $90 million endorsement deal with a high school student named

LeBron James was an extraordinary landmark for signing someone based on an *anticipated* future career. James has already achieved greatness with the National Basketball Association's Cleveland Cavaliers, and rejuvenated the entire city of Cleveland at the same time. Celebrity endorsements can also be very fickle, they can change like the wind—in a much publicized event James left Cleveland for Miami devastating that franchise.

Other solid examples of celebrity endorsement are the Michael Jordan and Nike collaboration, which led to the sale of the iconic Air Jordans, and Newman's Own, actor Paul Newman's line of organic food products. Newman's Own not only capitalizes on the nostalgia of old-school Hollywood glamour, but also encompasses the man's philanthropic lifestyle by donating a portion of all sales to charity. The best endorsement deals manage to equate the product with the appeal of the celebrity. Successful celebrity branding transfers the value of the person to the product he or she endorses.

 ### How Do You Argue with the Heavyweight Champion of the World?

Even great spokespersons have their moments. During production of the first show with George, we shot the first scene and he did a great job. However, there was a technical issue—I believe a sound problem—so I told him we had to do it again. He said, "I already gave you my best effort. I'm not going to do it again." I tried to explain to him that it wasn't him, it was a technical problem. But he wouldn't budge and refused to do another take. How do you argue with the heavyweight champion of the world?

With the proliferation of cameras on phones, and entities like celebrity news web site TMZ—not to mention the ever-present paparazzi—a Nike athlete caught in a candid shot on the way to the gym wearing another shoe brand might get "busted."

Again, that's the main reason George was so perfect for the grill. The Foreman and Salton shows for the grill let viewers see beyond Foreman's celebrity status and understand the actual lifestyle, which included the grill for health and convenience.

This cooperative endorsement deal skyrocketed Salton to the top of the household product makers, and the arrangement paid off for both parties. Foreman branched off on his own business ventures. Similar to Paul Newman's venture, a portion of all sales will go to Foreman's own charity, the George Foreman Youth & Community Center in Houston, Texas.

Grilling Up Some Big Numbers

It didn't take long for Foreman's face to become synonymous with indoor grilling. Since its debut in 1994 (it lived as a taco maker until 1996), the indoor grill has become one of the most popular household items of all time. It is estimated that somewhere between 12 and 15 percent of all U.S. households have *at least* one George Foreman Grill. It has nearly become, like toasters or blenders, one of those items that every single household considers essential for a complete kitchen.

The initial deal that was negotiated with Foreman was done between Leon Driemann, the CEO of Salton, and Sam Perlmutter, Foreman's agent and attorney. The contract gave Foreman 50 percent of the net profits on every grill that was sold. That meant if the retail price was $59.95, and the stores bought it for wholesale at $30, and the product cost was $15, he would get $7.50 for each grill sold. We were selling hundreds of thousands a month, so that got to be a pretty healthy number.

The deal that grabbed the headlines, however, was what Salton paid Foreman in 2000 to buy him out of this initial deal: $120 million in cash and another $10 million in Salton stock. At the time, it was the largest athletic endorsement deal ever. It was later reported that the total buyout deal was worth $137.8 million to Foreman, plus $23.8 million in stock. Foreman won't say how much he has made as a product endorser, but he doesn't dispute a published estimate that his lifetime earnings are about $240 million—three times what he earned in the ring.

In the first 10 years, nearly 20 million of the various George Foreman grilling machines had been sold. The countertop unit produced sales of approximately $200 million within four years. Total company sales rose to about $99 million, by 1996. Revenue then soared to $182 million in 1997. By 1998, Salton's revenue soared to more than $305 million, and roughly half the company's sales were brought in by products marketed through infomercials that were created by Cesari Direct. We made more than 14 different versions of various George Foreman infomercials.

In 2002 alone, worldwide sales catapulted the household grilling product to over $375 million. This led Salton to design a string of other Foreman-endorsed grilling products, including the George Foreman Champ Grill with Bun Warmer and the George Foreman Rotisserie. Foreman became the iconic grill-master, constantly on television cooking up sizzling department stores sales.

In 2007, Applica Inc. acquired Salton, and with it the George Foreman brand. Applica and George Foreman Cooking continue to add to the George Foreman Grill lineup, with several products from outdoor and indoor fat-reducing grills to blenders and broilers. Once the market was saturated, however, the company never again achieved the sales it enjoyed during earlier years.

OxiClean®

"Powered by the Air You Breathe, Activated by the Water You Drink"

By the mid to late 90s, of course, my company was regularly handling more than a dozen different direct response television product launches a year. I talk here about the most recognizable, because these are the projects people ask me about the most.

It was early in 1997 when I first met Joel Appel. It was his father, Max Appel, who had developed the all-natural cleaning products their company manufactured and distributed. Although Max wasn't a chemist or a product researcher, he had spent the early part of the 1980s experimenting with natural cleaning products. He had done so out of a genuine concern for people's health and the environment. He was intentionally working toward a goal of finding equally effective ways to clean house with nontoxic products.

Appel and his wife, Elaine, maintained their full-time jobs while building their small business and caring for their four growing children. In his garage in Littleton, Colorado, he experimented with all kinds of natural ingredients. His search eventually led him to explore a range of essential oils. He started looking at these oils because a few plant-based oils were already common ingredients in certain household cleaning products. Think about Lemon Pledge.

What he discovered in initial tests was that orange oil offered some interesting possibilities. Orange oil is a slightly sticky, oily substance, similar in consistency to that of turpentine. It was well known to have some rather effective cleaning properties, while still being all natural and nontoxic.

After much trial and error and, according to one interview, only minimal damage to a few of his kitchen cabinet doors, Appel devised a cleaning product that worked yet was entirely free of harsh solvents or toxic petrochemicals. The first thing he created was a wood cleaner and polish, which ended up containing the oil of 78 Valencia oranges *per bottle*. So aside from being all natural and nontoxic, the wood cleaner also had a refreshing orange scent that reinvigorated whatever area of the house had just been cleaned.

Then, starting in 1986, Appel sold the wood cleaner to friends and acquaintances. He and his wife were still working full-time, until they felt certain the company would succeed. Initially, Max was in charge of mixing and making the product, and was dubbed the "sales specialist"; Elaine managed all other operations— packaging, orders, and shipping. They finally recognized that their business would "make it" when Elaine had to leave her regular job one afternoon—"claiming a family emergency," she says—in order to fill customer orders waiting at home.

The business grew by baby steps. Before long, they were selling a variety of items, such as carpet sweepers and house- hold cleansers, at home shows and state fairs across the United States and Canada. This is the same kind of approach we took with our coast-to-coast Juiceman seminars.

The Appels' one-on-one interactions with customers proved to be just as invaluable to them as our experience during the Juiceman seminars. Loyal customers around the country offered advice for product refinement, new product uses, and thoughts on new products they could use. It was one of those personal suggestions that led Max Appel to develop a multipur- pose, degreaser for the product family, in 1988. Sales gradually increased, and growing social awareness of environmentally safe products helped keep sales moving steadily up.

In 1992, Max, Elaine, and their son Joel (who had become a marketing executive for Quaker Oats) each invested $10,000 and reincorporated the company as Orange Glo International. They made clear plans for expanding the company's market share.

The first step, in 1992, was to introduce Orange Glo to a small range of retail grocery stores. By 1995, the company was generating annual sales of $700,000 through retailers, direct mail sales, and fairs and home shows.

The company's first quantum leap occurred in 1996, when the Home Shopping Network (HSN) featured Orange Glo Wood Cleaner & Polish with a then relatively unknown pitchman named Billy Mays. The initial Home Shopping segment quickly boosted sales. During that first broadcast, the Appels sold out their entire inventory (4,000 bottles). After a few months of HSN sales, income grew to about $300,000 per month, almost *five times* as much as the previous sales year.

In 1997, the Orange Glo company introduced an organic stain and odor remover called OxiClean. When the OxiClean crystals were added to warm water, tiny oxygen bubbles traveled to the stain and forced the organic stain matter, such as wine, coffee, or dirt, to let go of fabrics. OxiClean's oxidation process made dirt disappear from the demonstration carpet as if by magic, without scrubbing.

Max, Joel, and the Orange Glo team decided to investigate DRTV to determine whether that model could help them accomplish their long-term goals. Joel recognized, much like the son of Vitamix inventor W.G. Barnard had done in 1949, that television was the way to get his father's product "out of the garage" and into the real world. The Appels actively sought our expertise at Cesari Direct. They really liked what we had done for a comparable cleaning product called Quick n Brite.

The story of how we finally met and decided to do an infomercial is a funny one, which I related to you in Chapter 2.

The Ubiquitous Billy Mays

It's impossible to think of Orange Glo, especially OxiClean, without thinking of Billy Mays. Tragically, Mays passed away in 2009; the funeral was held in his hometown of McKees Rocks, Pennsylvania. He was buried wearing a shirt with the OxiClean logo on it.

Despite the sadness of his death, it brought back some wonderful early memories to me of my experiences with the most notable "thumbs-up" man in the direct response business. I got to know Mays before his booming voice, beard, and blue shirt had made him an international icon. I can tell you that he was a decent, hard-working man, on and off the set, long before he became the most recognized television salesperson in history.

Like a lot of pitchmen in the direct response field, Mays started his career doing live pitches on the boardwalk of Atlantic City. He learned how to sell from the older, more experienced veteran salesmen there while he was growing up. Mays even attributed some of his unique flair to their influence.

In addition to his work in Atlantic City, Mays, like my first spokesman Jay Kordich, spent over a decade traveling to home shows and state fairs across the country. Mays and rival fair and expo salesman Max Appel met at the Pittsburgh home show in 1993. Mays sold a variety of products over the years, from hand tools to cleaning products to food choppers. Over the months and years, as their paths crossed at other shows, the two became friends.

In 1996, Appel hired Mays to sell his family's line of household cleaners, OxiClean and Orange Glo, on air for the Home Shopping Networks. There was an enthusiastic response by consumers to Mays's iconic style. Sales jumped immediately. Therefore, when the time came to get the infomercial off the ground, we decided that Billy Mays was perfect to be the spokesperson for OxiClean. His state fair and HSN experience meshed extremely well with this particular product line, making him the ideal representative for it. One thing we can take credit for is launching Mays's career on TV. We produced the very first OxiClean infomercial featuring him as "The Pitchman," in 1996.

The development of the show was practically a no-brainer for us. To be honest, it was one of the easiest shows we ever did. Easy for us because between Appel and Mays, they had years and years of practice and expertise selling products at state fairs and on HSN. They had pretty much refined their pitches over years of trial and error and came up with the most effective product demos and efficient ways to engage people emotionally with the products.

To this day, when an inventor brings a new product to us, I recommend they get real consumer feedback, either from direct sales at state fairs or a web site. This direct consumer feedback is much more valuable to creating a successful pitch than any focus group can be. The reason is, you are asking people to decide with their pocketbooks whether they truly liked the product and the pitch. They are giving you real money. In a focus group, people are only giving opinions.

Mays had already done all the hard work of developing and refining the highly successful perfect pitch for OxiClean. He knew exactly what to say to sell the product; and, of course, no one could captivate an audience as effectively in order to deliver the information to a receptive viewer. As a production company, all we had to do was turn on the cameras and let Mays do his thing. You can see Mays's original infomercial on our company web site www.cesaridirect.com.

The biggest problem we had with the first show was getting Mays's co-host, Kara Cox, to actually say something. I think she was overwhelmed with Billy's style and booming voice; plus, Billy was not used to working with a "sidekick." Sometimes, as much as 10 minutes would go by without Cox uttering a word. Finally, I offered to give her a $20 bill every time she would say something or react to what Mays had just demonstrated.

Coming "prepared to sell" was one of Mays's greatest attributes. When you worked with him on a project, no matter what it was, he wrote his own sales pitch. Among his many trademarks were the memorable catchphrases he originated. He created them for *all* the products he pitched in a way that was unique to him. For Orange Clean, he came up with "Great cleaning products *do* grow on trees," as a funny way to highlight the all-natural ingredients. He also devised, "When you need the muscle without the tussle" and "It's the cleaner that works, so you don't have to," to focus in on the *power* of the product despite its all-natural ingredients.

These shows featured a high-energy Billy Mays who brought a hard-sell style to both the 2-minute and 30-minute infomercials. The long-form infomercial was the perfect venue for Orange Glo products *and* Billy Mays. Demonstrating the stain-removing power of the products in a giant see-through aquarium, Mays provided compelling on-screen product demonstrations. The visual impact of the product in use—practically "dissolving" notoriously difficult stains such as blood, red wine, and embedded grass—was convincing.

For OxiClean, Mays invented, "Powered by the air we breathe, activated by the water you drink" to describe the origin of the chemical reaction that made it work. He didn't stop there. He also concocted, "Its Mother Nature approved" and "It's like a white knight in shining armor," to stress the ecologically sound ingredients and the product's efficacy. Few people can come up with and write funny, engaging, remarkably on-target one-liners the way Mays did.

 One of a Kind

Ron Lynch, my partner at Cesari Direct and coauthor of this book, once told me how Mays "got even" a few years ago with the executives at Taco Del Mar, a Seattle-based restaurant chain. Apparently, in an effort to boost sales, the chain ran an ad that was essentially a spoof on Billy Mays. It hired an actor to imitate Mays in an ad pushing Taco Del Mar burritos, without his permission. The ad succeeded in boosting sales, and that's when Mays thought he'd have some fun in return. He planned a payback routine, with the help of the chain's VP.

Mays stormed corporate headquarters, Michael Moore guerilla style. He had a fake cameraman and entire "news" crew that stood by filming as he launched a string of rapid-fire questions at the company's CEO. Mays grilled the poor man about the chain's taco sales and marketing techniques, and kept at it until the CEO got jumpy and nervous and started searching for a way out. Only then did Mays explode in his own patented brand of laughter as he explained the hoax and put the CEO out of his misery.

Mays's other characteristic, one that most people *didn't* see, was the "switch" he flipped on the second the camera started rolling. This shifted him immediately into high gear. I've only seen a few really successful entertainers able to accomplish this as effectively as Mays. Off camera, he was quieter; but once the cameras started rolling, watch out. This, I think, is the best compliment I can give him: He was a great, old-fashioned pitchman, the kind that just aren't around anymore.

Billy Mays's iconic voice simultaneously motivated response and successfully built brand loyalty. It closed the gap between brand and response. The investment paid off in sales for Orange Glo, which increased to $2 million *per month*.

All in all, my company ended up doing more than 10 long-form infomercials and several short-form spots for Orange Glo International products; OxiClean, Orange Glo Wood

Cleaner & Furniture Polish, KABOOM Shower, Tub & Tile Cleaner, and Orange Clean Degreasing Foam were just a few.

Very similar to the way Jay Kordich helped build the Juiceman brand, in my opinion, without Billy Mays as a spokesperson, Orange Glo would not have the success it enjoyed. His unique ability to pitch built a cleaning empire.

After the sale of Orange Glo, Mays's career continued to skyrocket, as he became a highly sought-after pitchman. He appeared in subsequent commercials for a number of "As Seen on TV" style products, which he reportedly used personally. His wife, Deborah, has said that he "believed in every product he sold, and he loved nothing more than bringing helpful products to people at a great savings."

In December of 2008, Mays began appearing in short spots for ESPN's online service, ESPN360 (now ESPN3). These ads had a slightly different flair than his usual fare. They were designed to parody his regular work in infomercials, with a heavy use of clichés. In essence, Mays was doing a parody of himself, and I'm sure he was in on the joke.

In the early part of 2009, Mays and his long-time friend and DRTV producer Anthony Sullivan developed a documentary series for the Discovery Channel called *PitchMen*. The show tagged along behind Sully and Mays as they accomplished their work in the direct response marketing field. After his death, the Discovery Channel broadcast a special Billy Mays tribute episode of the series called "Pitchman: A Tribute to Billy Mays."

Billy Mays's passing leaves behind a huge void that no one besides Mays himself seems to be able to fill. Several of his ads are still being broadcast (with his family's permission). Response rates are, in some cases, better than before his death. The feeling is, he would have wanted it that way.

Now that the home show and fair circuit has declined considerably, it's unlikely that a talent on par with that of Billy Mays will ever come along again. He will truly be missed.

The Rise of OxiClean

OxiClean was an unknown product when our firm took it on, with no advertising budget and no presence on retail shelves. The infomercials we made with Billy Mays pitted OxiClean head to head against the top brands in its category, including Tide, Cheer, and Clorox. Yet OxiClean managed to emerge victorious. You can attribute this to the power of the infomercial!

Traditionally, the fast-moving consumer goods industry (the category cleaning products fall under) resisted using direct response for a long time. Those originally managing these kinds of products preferred to build brand recognition with "creative" ads that attempted to establish an emotional connection without directly engaging the customer in any way. Hence, the viral jingles and cutesy catchphrases like, "Please don't squeeze the Charmin." Long ago, marketers had unanimously decided that this type of product (fast-moving consumer goods) wasn't suited to direct response. It was through the success of OxiClean that the old paradigm was shattered, proving once and for all that there is more than one way to position fast-moving consumer goods.

Between 1997 and 1999, Orange Glo International managed to acquire shelf space for its products in regional and national chains, including Target, Walmart, Sam's Club, Walgreens, Costco, and others. As OxiClean moved into stores, major players like Clorox and P&G also tried selling their products through infomercials. It seems the success of the OxiClean DR campaign irrevocably established direct response as another way to market conventional consumer products. One of the benefits of this success was that retailers shed their initial reluctance to carrying direct response products. Some national heavyweights such as Walgreens not only have embraced these products in their stores, they have devoted entire front-of-store sections to

"As Seen on TV" items. But it all started with Orange Glo and OxiClean. These were the products that shattered the belief that fast-moving consumer goods couldn't be marketed directly to consumers.

Within two short years, by October 2000, Orange Glo ranked number four on *Inc.* magazine's list of the 500 fastest-growing private companies, with $86 million in revenues. That means, between 1995 and 1999, Orange Glo revenues increased by more than *11,000 percent.*

Unique Packaging Strategy

There were two elements that really helped us accelerate direct sales. The first that was new to this campaign was multiproduct packages. OxiClean and Orange Glo benefitted from a unique packaging strategy that was perfect for the company's products and customers.

Since Max Appel had continued developing cleaning products, with the help of consultants, Orange Glo was able to organize a set of household cleaning products in a way that offered incredible convenience to consumers. Some of these new products included Orange Clean Foam & Degreaser, for cleaning greasy dirt; Power Paste; Bar of Oranges hand and body soap; Orange Grove Air Freshener; and Orange for Hands, a heavy-duty liquid soap.

The company also began offering environmentally friendly cleaning tools, such as terry-cloth mops, magnetized brooms, and squeegee cloths. Combining a few key tools with a set of core products was an unbeatable combination for consumers. They could get practically all their household cleaning needs from one convenient, earth-friendly source.

The possibilities for combination product packages grew in 2000 when Orange Glo introduced the KABOOM brand of household cleaning products. As with all other Orange Glo products, the KABOOM line was also distributed to retail stores and sold via infomercials. Orange Glo was able to fully capitalize on all its products this way. This is one of the characteristics of great management I'm referring to when I say that a company I've worked with has attained the triple crown of potential success. It is when a small company manages to get all three of the most important aspects of its business operating dynamically.

First of all, triple crown companies offer an excellent product. Next, they develop highly successful advertising for that product. And, third, they put smart businesspeople at the helm. The Appels were savvy leaders and were, therefore, able to convert that initial blush of success into tremendous long-term growth. Sonicare and Rug Doctor were the other companies we worked with that had all three in place. It is no coincidence that all of these companies sold for hundreds of millions of dollars!

One of the strategies that contributed to the dynamic growth and success of Orange Glo was not only to package its products into cleaning systems and value kits, but to cyclically reorganize the product quantities or types for different situations. The fact that all the products were *natural* cleaning products, as were the cleaning accessories such as mops and sponges, only strengthened consumer loyalty. The convenience could only be made simpler and more convenient one way: *continuity programs*.

"Continuity" literally means uninterrupted in sequence or succession. A continuity program provides an automated ongoing supply of the product in question to be delivered to the customer at specified intervals. The consumer's credit card is charged at each shipment. These kinds of direct sales programs had been in action since the days when encyclopedia salesmen went door to door, and the extensive collection was delivered over a course of months or years.

Time-Life offered a large variety of long-term continuity programs, delivering a series of 24 or 48 books or record albums of a "collection" over a periods time. There were classical musical collections, and book collections dedicated to topics like the history of the Wild West or of World War I or II. Cesari Direct introduced a continuity model to the OxiClean campaign that contributed to its sales explosion.

They say the true success of any new product can be measured in the number of imitators. If so, then Orange Glo was a hands-down success and, thus, a perceived threat to other major cleaning product manufacturers. Just about all these companies introduced a newer version of some well-known household products with the addition of orange scent or a diluted form of orange oil. Some such products included Pledge Furniture Polish with Orange Oil and Fantastik Orange Action All-Purpose Cleaner. Unlike Orange Glo, these competitors' products were not necessarily environmentally friendly. There's no doubt that many consumers of major-brand "orange" cleaning products likely *presumed* those products were also "green," or environmentally friendly, by association. Not only was Orange Glo benefiting from the incredible impact of the infomercials, other major brands were piggybacking on Orange Glo's and OxiClean's success.

No one is really surprised when an infomercial product, especially a great one, is "knocked off" by some fly-by-night imitators that prey on inattentive consumers. Inevitably, these copycats use lesser materials or ingredients in order to offer their knockoff product at prices significantly lower than the original. Often, before the complaints can even be voiced, these companies have pulled up roots and disappeared, leaving behind a trail of unhappy consumers. This is just a part of life in the infomercial business, and also one of the reasons a campaign must be carefully organized and twice as precisely executed.

At Cesari Direct, our experience provides us with the insight we need to narrow down our process to include the most efficient and most highly effective methods for each product's unique benefits. Of course, when Orange Glo's OxiClean products hit the ground running, and grew popular, national competitors were quick to get back into research and development to produce their own versions of oxygen-based products.

Orange Glo's OxiClean infomercial was the first of more than 12 different shows that introduced new products, including: KABOOM, Orange Clean, and Orange Glo Furniture Polish. We maintained a strategic mix of long- and short-form DRTV campaigns, timed to best suit new product introductions at the retail level. This DRTV approach ultimately generated sales in excess of $250 million for the company! In August 2006, Orange Glo International was sold for $325 million.

The Customer Is
No Dummy

A ll these years of marketing have led us to one basic conclusion that reigns as a rule over all our creative decisions at Cesari Direct. The key component in today's successful direct response campaign is *not* the product or service, at all. It is, in fact, the consumer. Think about the explosion of "reality" TV in the past decade. What is the common thread in reality TV programs? The participants are like us, complete with the flaws, imperfections, frailties, and follies of the common folk. When Carrie Underwood makes it from obscurity to stand on *American Idol*, belting her way to a million-dollar record deal and fame, millions of young girls are in front of their TVs saying, "That could be *me*." There is something very honest, raw, and compelling about viewing what we perceive to be "real." We feel that "reality" represents us. We like to watch "TV about me." Understanding this is simple, but one of the hardest concepts to build into what we in the business call a *creative*.

One of our media clients has a very successful show for a product called P90X. You've probably seen it. The creative is a compilation of consumer home videos touting the toughness of the exercise plan. Cesari Direct did not make the show, but we recognized the brilliance behind it was that it went against the grain of the exercise culture. That is, everybody else was making shows about how fun or easy their programs were; these guys flew in the face of that, bragging, "This is the toughest exercise program in the world. It will kick your butt." They backed it up with self-shot, low-production-value videos from user after user, including the founders of the program. They convince you that P90X is absolute torture. It feels very real. The results, however, are astonishing. You almost forget that the users didn't look so fat or bad before they started, because they turn out to be such chiseled Adonises and their female equivalents. The point we're making here is that because the P90X connects itself so directly to reality and honesty, the viewers think it has to be true. Consequently, the product is a huge success, a newly branded giant in fitness.

The most important lesson we have drawn from the rise of reality television is that the modern viewer is adept at distinguishing sincere, real-life human behavior from feigned. This can be a great obstacle for marketers. It means candid interviews must be candid. Testimonials must be real testimonials. There's just no faking it. We work very hard to make sure all of our campaigns are credible throughout. If the learned viewers' "BS" meter goes off, you're toast.

It is human nature when you are talking about a product to do just that: talk about the product and totally forget to involve the consumer. What we've learned to do is create a dialogue that's about the consumer *first*. Then we fold in the products as a clear solution to the problems of their lives. Often, our shows or ad spots start with some simple questions that help pull the viewers in and let them know that we want to speak to them. When done well, the questions are empathetic and direct.

One of the most important questions you have to ask as a marketer, from the start is, "Am I selling to men or women, or both?" The answer should determine the entire course of your communications. We have sufficiently proved to ourselves that there is a very profound and distinctive difference between how men and women tend to view a presentation or purchase.

This discussion is one we have frequently with clients, and it can be off-putting to some. We have proven to ourselves that women and men approach purchasing in very different ways. This has to do with the fact that their brains are wired differently. This is fodder for many comedians, but as we all know, most comedy contains an ounce (or more) of truth. More and more research shows that our basic view of the world is really shaped by having our brains marinated in either estrogen or testosterone during gestation and the first years of our lives.

Wow! Weren't expecting that in a marketing book were you?

Nonetheless, it's basically true. Men are single-focused hunters. Women are gatherers, with diffuse awareness. It was something we already knew as marketers but it was highlighted and put this concisely when we did an interview recently with relationship expert Alison Armstrong, whose research was confirmed by our good friend Dr. Daniel Amen, an expert on brain science. To be clear, neither of the following broad strokes is 100 percent true for everyone 100 percent of the time, but as a species the brains of men and women seem to have very different ways of collecting, filtering, and organizing information.

In more detail, men as hunters respond to paths that lead them places. They like to "acquire specific targets" and follow them. When they are busy focusing on something, they block out everything else. Can you say "televised sports"? Men are extremely linear. They seem to respond well to Pythagorean arguments— A + B = C, and the like. They respond to things called "sales arguments." They like conflict and resolution. They love winning. They follow pathlike order and linear thinking. Details do not seem as nearly as important to men as do results and finite solutions. I would go so far as to say, ultimately, they like intimidation and confrontation, as well. Men are the ones who say, "Oh yeah?! Then *prove* it." If you can prove it, they tend to be more open to a buying decision. If you can get a man's attention—and that can be a pretty big "if" sometimes—they are often easier to sell to than women. They will follow your breadcrumbs, as long as you don't treat them like idiots. They are not stupid, but they are easy to lead through a linear television pitch—if you can hold their attention. Many of our shows for car products are targeted at males and rely on chemical experiments, pretty girls, lots of fast camera shots, fire, flashiness, and rock 'n' roll. This works for men!

Women, conversely, seem to respond more to sales "dialogues," as opposed to arguments. They prefer that you stand next to them and make observations with them about the perils of the world. Women hate being criticized, though they are highly self-critical. Criticism and intimidation do not work; conferring does. There is not much of a need for "proof" or experimentation with women. Simple before-and-afters really are appealing to them. Hearing from "real" women in candid conversations, describing both the negative and the positive effects of a product, is crucial. Even in focus groups, when faced with evaluating testimonials, women claim that "all the women are actresses." Nevertheless, they still need to hear from them. The order of presentation also seems to matter less to women, as they tend to hear the parts of the story that apply to them and disregard the rest. They can "connect the dots" much better than men. What women really do appreciate is the constant addition of new and different information. The number-one complaint women have about long-form infomercials is their repetitive nature. Dynamic television is more valuable to them. Their intuitive nature allows them to make abstract connections.

The unfortunate reality is that so many products appeal to both men and women that you *have* to be repetitive, so that men *hear* the information, because their single focus is being broken by women getting more information. There was a comedian a few years back who joked, "Men have to be told everything three times before they hear it. That's why all those signs say, 'LIVE, LIVE, LIVE, GIRLS, GIRLS, GIRLS.'" There's more than an ounce of truth in that.

To a man, a good sales pitch is like a good arrow: It gets to the meat—short, straight, and to the point. It actually may leave some things unanswered. To a woman, a good pitch is more like a good basket: woven, connected, and three-dimensional. It needs to hold more water.

Positioning Your Product: The Next Niche

I am a voracious reader. I read a couple of books a week outside of my 60- to 90-hour-a-week work schedule. Airplanes and hotels offer me the opportunity to do this, along with a Kindle. There have been a number of books that when "connected," have really added to the dynamic success we've enjoyed at Cesari Direct.

When I first read Napoleon Hill's *Think and Grow Rich*, my eyes were opened to a new kind of thinking, which allowed me to break free of a whole host of character traits that, unconsciously, had kept me from realizing my potential. Selfishness, fear, and envy were probably the biggest ones that I have had to work on my whole life. I have spent much energy and effort trying to prove to myself that I can escape these common basic frailties that Hill discusses. His work is probably the single most-endorsed piece of literature I have ever come across. Every single mega-successful person I've met or interviewed over the years at some point cites this particular book as the moment the lightbulb went on for them. Many of the passages in Hill's work highlighted for me things that I internally knew to be true. I just had not acknowledged them before. If you have not read the book, do.

Tony Robbins came along to the direct response world in the late 1980s as a big-hit seminar "product" for Guthy-Renker. Robbins had done something brilliant: He built on what Napoleon Hill had started, then aggregated more and more similar material from other authors and personal coaches, developing an easy CD/DVD seminar series, with books to support. His information was not entirely unique, but he had done the work, added his own salt and pepper and packaged it in a wrapper that was easily digestible for millions. When I first read *Unlimited Power*, the book included with Robbins's seminar, I was impressed with this guy who confirmed and highlighted so many things that we at Cesari Direct already were doing that had made us so successful—things, again, I had not acknowledged. Another book worth reading, if you have not.

This déjà vu happened to me one more time, in 2006, when I ran into my former creative director and coauthor of this book, Ron Lynch. Ron and I had met years before when he worked as a manager in a local grocery store in my neighborhood. He was always bright, polite, and very funny. He became an acquaintance I could rely on anytime I needed to shoot an ad in a supermarket! Over the years he had grown into a consulting job, working for independent grocers doing "turnarounds," helping stores go from "losing money" to "making money." Mind you, I grew up in the grocery business and knew the business acumen it took to succeed in that net 1 percent industry. It's a brutal business environment for chains, let alone independents. One day I heard through the grapevine that he had quit his job and optioned a screenplay to my buddy Sam Perlmutter. One, I had no idea the guy could write. Two, I had no idea he was using my connections to further his career. I was a little taken back, but also pretty impressed. He was a true entrepreneur. I had a senior partner in our office contact him and we offered him a test gig writing a commercial for Space Bags. Ron ended up working for me for several years; he had a couple of great shows that lasted for five-plus years and sold products into the hundreds of millions of dollars. Understanding his adventurous nature and desire for growth, we parted as friends when he left to cut his teeth in more entrepreneurial endeavors in our industry.

Flashing forward to 2006, I ran into Ron at the International Home + Housewares Show in Chicago and learned he was doing very well—had many hit shows. I'm really proud of him.

In our conversation, he told me he had learned a couple of secrets in the past few years and was interested in working together. He also told me to read a book called *Blue Ocean Strategy: How to Create Uncontested Market Space and Make Competition Irrelevant*, and if I liked what I read, to give him a call. Timing is a funny thing: Max Appel had given me the same book about a month earlier, and I was very inspired by both the book and the fact that Ron saw its value to our business.

As it turns out, *Blue Ocean Strategy* is a very good book by W. Chan Kim and Renée Mauborgne from INSEAD Blue Ocean Strategy Institute, one of the top European business schools. In it, the authors describe the very same methodology we've been using at Cesari Direct for years. Again, we just hadn't acknowledged it. It wasn't that we were dumb, or smart; it just verified that our instincts had been very good and that the lessons we learned on the way to the top were very valuable. We'd just done it the hard way, before they wrote the book. One of the most important elements of the Blue Ocean Strategy is the concept that, as a company, you want to create uncontested market space, or "blue ocean," through differentiation. Once you have your own blue ocean, it's easier to sail and navigate without bumping into competitors. You realize you don't want to just push off and differentiate your product from the others; you need to take a deep dive and make sure your product does something that allows you to create a new category of products.

A business that starts a new category is very likely to go into the leadership of that space—fast. The second guy in gets less market share. The third guy in gets even less. So instead of running headlong into a sea of competition, create your own ocean.

We had done it so many times before. Surely, there were juicers for years before the Juiceman. We created the space of healing nutrition through the use of juice and raw foods. The

Juiceman just helped the consumer get to the goal. Certainly, countertop grills and sandwich presses had been around for decades. We made the George Forman Lean Mean Fat-Reducing Grilling Machine. The two-sided, grill-marked surface and the little slope that drained out the fat were the features we hung our hat on. Ours was the grill that cooked faster while lowering the fat content in the food. We knew how to make our own blue oceans; we did it with a tool we call the USP, the unique selling proposition.

I called Ron and agreed to make some more blue oceans for our clients. Today, Ron is a partner in our firm and a completely innovative strategic thinker; he shares my passion for this industry, and his love for the business enthuses our clients and generates real increases in sales for them.

Get to Your Unique Selling Proposition

It doesn't matter if you are a Fortune 500 company or an inventor in a garage, if you have any intention of finding success in direct response, you need a USP. There are 40,000 reasons why. Forty thousand is the number of marketing messages we, as consumers, are pummeled with every week in the United States. It is a staggering number, but we don't seem to notice. You want to be heard? You want to get past all that white noise? You gotta say something new; you gotta make it about me; and you've got about three seconds to do it before I tune you out. One of the best ways to do that is with the right question, an open-ended question the consumer must feel compelled to acknowledge.

One of the best, longest-running brand advertising bits of all time is the "Got Milk?" campaign by Goodby, Silverstein & Partners. The reason I love it so much is that it asks such a simple question that is widely accepted in the American home. The question engages you with the assumption that the product is so core to the running of your household that you must stop and think if you have any in the refrigerator. It's not, "Do you like milk?" "Wouldn't you love some fresh nutritious milk now?" It's "Got Milk?" Of course you need it! Are you out? It builds an immediate sense of urgency. At the same time, it opens up your subconscious to the possibility of why, and you instantly validate the need. Then, the whimsical nature of the question allows it to be paired with a million different images that reinforce all the reasons that consumers enjoy milk. Everything from fitness and muscles to warm chocolate chip cookies to a sexy milk bath—if it's associated with milk, the firm hit it. The first television ad they shot, in 1993, was directed by movie mogul Michael Bay and starred Sean Whalen as a listener to a radio contest call-in program trying to answer the question, "Who shot Patrick Henry? Foiled by a mouthful of peanut butter, he tries to eke out the name "Aaron Burr." Fantastic! In print, I've seen this now-famous ad question paired with babies, weightlifters, rock stars, athletes, actors, and even kittens. It works every time. A good marketing question engages consumers.

Once you've asked the right question, you have to be prepared to give an answer that distinguishes you and creates a new category through your USP, the unique selling proposition. What is it about your product that makes it unique? What's the thing that guarantees you will be the first "in" in a category to establish and hold the best long-term dominance? Here's an example of how this can work.

A few years ago, we were approached by the Hunter Fan Company, one of the oldest and most trusted companies in the country. Traditionally, Hunter had been known for making quality, quiet ceiling fans that lasted for years and years. You probably have one in your home. As we soon learned, Hunter was more than fans. The company had developed a whole range of products that expanded into lighting, automated "lights-on" systems, floor fans, air purifiers, and more. Recently, it had licensed a technology, a proven advancement in indoor air purification and safety. The technology was incredible; it was being used in the utmost secure government buildings to protect against acts of terror, including biological weapons.

Hunter's business problem was that to deliver a really great product to the consumer, the cost of production would be relatively high, compared to the category. The retail would be around $400. Further, the product had no retail presence and was about to jump into a fairly crowded field. The existing market for air purifiers was about $49 to $199. On television, we had all seen the success of David Oreck's air purifier, the Sharper Image Ionic Breeze Air Purifier, and the knockoff version, the Ionic Pro. There were lots of air purifiers in the early 2000s. How could we make the Hunter product different? What would be the USP?

Most of the air purifiers in the market were some form of electrostatic precipitator, or "ESP," technology. ESPs rely on a "blade" collector with a low-voltage current running through it that worked basically like a static generator. It would charge particles drawn in by a fan then collect them electrostatically on washable plates. This technology is most efficient at grabbing dust, dander, pollen, and the like. It does work—not incredible, but sufficient. The blades, however, get to be hard to clean over time.

Looking closely at the source of the technology in Hunter's device, we discovered that it had the capability to capture and kill biological material like germs, molds, bacteria, and viruses. The company had clinical data to clearly support the claims. They could kill relatives of anthrax and tuberculosis with this thing. Heck, the FBI put the same technology in Langley to protect from letter bombers and Al-Qaeda. This was good stuff. We had our distinct difference, but how could we gently make the point without scaring people?

It was a subtle shift. We decided we would not sell against the other air purifiers out there. In fact, we'd highlight them in our show, even complement them for being good enough at collecting dust, dander, and pollen. Then we asked a simple question: "Is 'good enough' really good enough for your family? Sure, you can protect from dust and pollen, but what about colds, flus, and airborne germs that cause sickness?"

We made a conscious decision to create a new category *above* air purification, one with a stronger name that implied greater efficacy. We called it "air sterilization." We explained that instead of ESP technology, Hunter had something new that was better. It actually used a modified form of HEPA filtration, a fabric or paper barrier filter that traps particulates. The novelty was that within this filter was embedded an electrostatic coil that charged the surface of the filter. Think of a bug zapper on steroids. This thing killed over 99.9 percent of the biological material it trapped.

We went after the most honest and trusted spokesperson we could think of, Peggy Fleming. She refused to do the show until she had seen and read all the material we could provide, and was adequately convinced that the device was the real McCoy. She ordered two units six weeks before shooting, and after experiencing the benefits, agreed to host.

Our USP was simple: We were the world's first in a new category of devices called air sterilizers, a technology that certainly did what older air purifiers and filters did—collect pollen, dust, and dander—but that went further, capturing and killing the bacteria, viruses, and germs that can make people sick. Colds, flus, and the like were in our crosshairs. The implication that the product could not just influence allergen issues, but mitigate airborne pathogens as well, gave it a unique launching point and story about clean, healthy home air. That made it stand out in the marketplace.

Technology can be very compelling, but it is not the only path to take to discover your USP. Ideally, your USP will lead you to the creation of a new category. This is not necessary for success, but it can certainly increase your ability to penetrate the market, tell a fresh story, and boost the ultimate value of your enterprise upon exit.

To find your USP, first list your imagined competitors' products, and write down every good aspect they have. This is a pain-producing exercise that will take all of your maturity and intestinal fortitude. Of course, you think the competitor is crap; that's why you bought this book. But set your ego aside for a minute and list how great your competitors are.

Now go ahead and list the ways they fall down on the job. Yes, I know you will enjoy this part, but it too has a purpose. Next, list your points of favor, line by line, next to those of your competitors. Now your product's weaknesses—it has some; write them down. Remember, you are on the search for uniqueness here. You want to find a way to say I can be in a different business than they are. Sure, you may have some similar customers, but if you create your USP correctly, you may find that their customers will move to your product on apparent innovation.

The goal of the USP is to create a blue ocean. Don't "BS" yourself on this. If you cannot find a clear way to create a definite USP, you should probably change the product or service. It takes just as much blood, sweat, and tears to market a failure as a success. If you can't convince a total stranger that you have a brand-new product that he or she has never experienced before, you do not have a business that will be viable. You are just a me-too. I'm sure you know the carpenter's adage: Measure twice, cut once. If you have no way to measure that your product is worthwhile, move on.

Now, let's say you are an inventor, and you have achieved the dream in your own eyes. Find a way to survey some intelligent people—no one you are related to! People who are related to inventors are used to telling them how great they are because they typically won't stand for it any other way.

Go find some intelligent strangers. Use the Internet. Get a second, a third, and a fourth opinion before you go from prototype to market hype. The reason? Let me illustrate. Here are some of the "mass market" products inventors have brought to me in the past:

- The dog water bowl: A 10-inch porcelain dog bowl shaped like a toilet—because all dogs like drinking from the toilet.
- The $5,000 "chopper": A 6,000 BTU custom motorcycle-style barbeque. Kid Rock built it himself, and it was truly awesome. But who can afford it?
- The $14,500, four-minute workout machine: No idea how many of these monsters they sell, but they still advertise in in-flight magazines.
- Automatic footy dispenser: Stick in your foot, pull it out and you have a painter's booty on your shoe to keep your home safe from dirty shoes. Also gives you that "ER" look around the house.
- The waffle iron keyboard: Just what you need, waffles in the shape of your desktop keyboard!
- The Kegel exercise program: Not kidding. This was an exercise program designed to strengthen your core through internal pressure exercises on the pelvic region. Good luck with that on mainstream television.

And everybody's favorite . . .
- Men's padded undergarments: To enhance the fullness of your appearance (in the front).

Now, I poke a little fun, but all of the people who brought these to me had actual products. The inventors were talented, and the designs were valid. They all worked. They were marketable. In fact, every one of these products achieved the goal to define and create a USP. But they were all lacking something for true market success: mass appeal. Generally, we have always operated under the safe assumption that the key to what we do is to find and market products that can be sold, or at least be marketed, to 80 percent of the public at large. This was not a guideline for us. It was a *rule*. Following this rule almost put us out of business.

Channel Explosion

The Next Paradigm Shift

At Cesari Direct, part of our operating philosophy has always been to sell products we felt good about selling. Whether we were selling food processors, juicers, or storage systems, we always wanted to sell things we would sell to our family members, with our heads held high. Our success came from picking low-hanging fruit. After all, every home should have a Juiceman, a George Forman Grill, and OxiClean. When there were only 40 television channels that made perfect sense. The reason being, the viewing audience were all in a very small corral. We just assumed it was big. We also believed that for an item to be successful in DR it had to be marketable to about 80 percent of America. What we eventually learned is that the explosion of cable to 400 or more stations reshaped the ability to precisely target smaller demographics.

A very interesting thing happened around 1998 or 1999: More and more unique channels started filling the cable space, and show performance declined across the board. Media companies were closing faster than Yugo dealerships. There still were hit shows, but the astronomically successful airings, where you'd spend $1,000 for a half hour and sell $7,000 worth of goods, were drying up. Companies blamed show producers, producers blamed media agencies, media agencies blamed stations for gouging prices. And I considered I might just sell the shop and go back to the beach.

I muddled on, though, and the industry struggled as a whole. People who tell you it didn't are either liars or had one product that was on fire and dodged the bullet for the time being. Then came 9/11.

I remember my phone ringing at 6:40 in the morning. It was my sister-in-law telling me to turn on my television.

She was hysterical and completely inconsolable. I hung up the phone, hit the power button on the remote, and stood in my living room, frozen in place by the sight of the pillar of smoke coming out of World Trade Center North. I honestly thought when they said "plane," they meant a Cessna. I looked at the hole in the building and thought it had to be a Cessna with a bomb. Then I watched as plane number two came in to view. It was no Cessna. I remember tears running down my cheeks, and feeling utter disbelief at what I was witnessing. This was no accident.

The next few years were interesting. We noticed a shift in what was working, from a television aspect. All of our home improvement products, cooking products, exercise, and comfort products worked. Nothing else did. People were nesting. Eating out less. Staying home more. Web sales were creeping up and up. More and more stations were added monthly, and low media rates were gone forever. Broadcast and cable television stations now received up to 40 to 45 percent of their revenue from direct response marketers. They figured out what we'd known all along: This is the most powerful advertising possible. Our model was shifting, others were skimming our profits, and we needed to figure something out—fast.

One morning, we got a call from a friend in the industry who was a consultant to a variety of companies. He told us about an affiliation with a company that had a product proven to work in direct response, a product that needed a second wind; but the company was just not sure how to execute. The product was a very good countertop hydroponic-like garden, branded as AeroGarden, by AeroGrow International, Inc. The company had run a 30-minute show for a year or two and had sold in the hundreds of thousands.

Now, truthfully, I have two plants in my office; I water them both, and despite my travel schedule manage to keep them alive, with no assistance. That is the full extent of my gardening career. I've always traveled too much for gardening, yet as an admitted juice junky and massive produce eater, I am supporter of the practice! We do have a number of dedicated gardeners in the office, including Ron, so thankfully I had help.

For three or four days, our team sat and poured over the existing successful marketing of the product. We looked at the intelligence the company had gained from the consumers who bought. We looked at the web traffic and marketing. We evaluated the media channels where the greatest success was found. We looked at the messaging, the USP, even the assortment of the seed pods AeroGrow sold in its razor-blade model.

Then, suddenly, we had a revelation that shifted our thinking and changed the way we will market, forever.

You see, the product worked pretty well on this explosion of new cable channels, including cooking channels, women's interest channels, gardening channels, and home improvement/do-it-yourself channels. Do you know what all those channels' viewers have in common? (Remember, assume you know nothing.) What do they have in common? Drum roll . . . Not a cotton pickin' thing. Nothing. They are all radically different demographics, quantifiably different customers. Epiphany.

Direct Demographic Media Messaging

Here's the lesson that came to us out of the explosion of media channels: As marketers, we are trained, or innately develop, a sales argument or pathlike dialogue. At Cesari Direct, we had learned to defeat the writing style that being men dictates. We learned how to write based on emotional triggers; multiple narratives, to speak to audiences; even words that appeal more to women or men, depending on the product. What we had *not* learned was how to escape the paradigm of traditional mass advertising messaging. We were stuck in a world where we created a campaign to grab the attention of the most valuable segment or two of consumers that fit the purchasing profile and demographics of a product. If you got the top tier or two of customers, you had supposedly maximized your potential. AeroGarden proved that model was completely inaccurate and archaic, and was limiting sales. We were about to go in a new direction for our clients, to start down a road and create something called *Direct Demographic Media Messaging*.

A great product or service has a number of different consumers, who buy it for a multiplicity of reasons. Direct Demographic Media Messaging allows multiple prioritized messages to be delivered to a variety of consumers through matched media channels. Unique messaging by viewer interest and media channel that returns identifiable sales for every media dollar spent is the goal—particularly in short-form media.

What we do today is a new science within the realm of direct response advertising, one that is more precise at every level. Through Direct Demographic Media Messaging, we identify unique compelling messages about your product; prioritize the messages in a unique order for different vertical demographic segments within your customer group; then cultivate a brand-connected direct response marketing campaign that is placed in specific media channels on television, radio, online, and electronically, where that particular vertical demographic resides. We present a value proposition and offer then demand a consumer action: Pick up the phone and call; go to the web and order.

Traditionally, when you approach a DR product launch, you have finite funds. It's just a fact. You are not sending out a message to a 100 million existing Nike fans who already have insight to your brand. You are seeking to convert the masses to your product, which most likely has never been heard of before. You don't have 10 million bucks, even if you are a Fortune 500. Even *they* don't risk that kind of money. So, you figure, I'm only going to get a few swings here at the piñata: How am

I going to bust it open? Thus ensues the traditional brand version of the "normal process."

You get in a room with your best five or six people and two or three from the ad agency. You whip out a spreadsheet and start ticking off the market sizes and shares you got from either your own geek or an outside corporate geekdom. You measure demographics. You understand that 60 percent of customers are female. They stratify across age groups in a bell-shaped curve that always seems to belly out at 45- to 55-year-olds, with a strong skew favoring the 55- to 70-year-olds over the 18- to 35-year-olds. You even can tell they watch *Oprah*. Wow! Now you know your target. If you could just get on *Oprah*. . . . So far, everything is falling into place. Only one problem. That chart looks the same as every single one in every other boardroom in America; and, yes, if you can get Oprah to say she loves your product, you will look like a genius. Next.

So you move to stage two. Individual consumer data: Who likes this kind of product? What do they do? Where do they shop? Do they identify as a Starbucks customer or a Peet's customer? Costco or Target? There are so many choices.

Now you make a list of the demographic you are pretty sure represents the biggest school of fish you want in your net. You create a series of messages that are sure to get them. These will be your low-hanging fruit. Then you get on to the "second tier"; you message to them. You don't go too much farther, because your message starts to get a little schizophrenic and you sound like you are trying to be all things to all people. Which you are. Your message has now become the white noise itself, instead of standing out above it.

Messaging versus Demographic

To highlight how this usually works, consider the following chart that represents typical messaging versus demographic.

For this example, let's consider that we are marketing a small countertop food processor. It has many features that will be communicated as benefits to the consumer. Let's assume that we have done a significant market survey to discover who is most likely to purchase the device, and which of its features they see the most benefit in. Across the top are groups A through E, in descending market group sizes. We'll ignore other factors, like average household income, race, and so on, for this example. We'll just assume that we have good intelligence that lets us know that group A is the ideal "biggest pool."

	A	B	C	D	E
	Female 36–45, Married: 70%	Female 46–55, Married: 65%	Male 35–55, Married: 60%	Seniors 55+ Married: 50%	Male and Female 24–35, Married: 35%
Small; handy	1	6	5	4	1
Makes meals fast	2	1	1	1	3
Easy to clean	3	2	5	5	2
Versatile	4	3	2	9	4
Powerful	5	7	3	10	8
Makes small portions	6	5	7	2	9
Dishwasher safe	7	10	8	3	5
Lifetime warranty	8	4	4	7	7
Quiet	9	8	9	6	6
White color	10	9	10	8	10

Down the left side of the chart are the traits or features of the device, ranked in preference by group A, your core target consumer. The rest of the columns show how other segments rate the same features. You will, of course, tie these to benefits when you construct a sales argument.

Looking at the other potential groups that may find value in the product, you can see that their order of preference is highly jumbled. In a traditional ad model you would probably build a creative for groups A and B, generally ignoring the rest, or hoping they'd hear enough to build a bridge in their own minds.

The obvious conundrum is how to effectively communicate to group A while appealing to as many consumers in the other tiers as possible, to maximize your profitability. It is important to note that along with this effort, you will develop a media plan that puts your ad in front of consumers in group A, as well.

What we have learned at Cesari Direct is how to develop a creative strategy and media plan that work together to increase the chances of success with all these consumer groups. Under the conditions this chart presupposes, we would consider making a series of commercials, one execution per valid consumer category. The spots would all be tied together with a key concept and visuals to ensure the look and feel of a cohesive DR-branded campaign.

The logic starts with the fact that, to cover all the messages, you would need very similar principal photography. The cost differential in production is nominal, particularly when you go to market and measure acquisition. You rearrange the messaging to weigh heavier on the key messages as they pertain to each customer group. Then you would match them to the correct identifiable media outlet where that consumer segment is known to reside. You would then unify all the creatives by engaging the viewer with a question that is assumptive and engaging. In this case, you might launch a campaign with, "Hey, what's for dinner tonight?" It's a question we all ask every day, and gets us on the road to a solution we know we can provide to every customer segment. The answer, and its weight, will be driven by the consumers as they have defined themselves. Then each creative execution is married to a media plan that targets the group.

For instance, you might focus one spot on Lifetime and Oxygen channel-type media, to find married women 35 to 45. Other executions might land on the Food Network or Fox News, to pair with the consumer base of age and level of affluence.

The key to maintaining brand is tying together the cohesive look and feel of the spots to keep the brand and campaign intact. This ensures that as consumers cross channels and bump into the other executions, they can creatively connect the spots, improving the appearance of your brand as, perhaps, having a larger presence. Looking big and strong helps consumer confidence and reaction, even for mom-and-pops.

Returning to AeroGarden as the example, here's how this strategy manifested.

What Are You Going to Grow Today?

The AeroGarden is such a neat device. In it you can grow almost anything—tomatoes, herbs, flowers, even fresh peppers—right on your countertop. In our experience with AeroGarden, we grew something much more valuable: targeted strategy.

In our discovery, we learned that the original half-hour show sold, but didn't "live long." The show was discovered by a variety of different consumer segments, enthusiasts in radically different areas. They were avid gardeners, often men who wanted to grow stuff in the winter. They were moms who wanted to have a fresh herb garden on their counters, to clip some fresh basil onto frozen lasagna, to feel as though they had "cooked" a fresh meal. They were floral lovers who enjoyed having fresh flowers on display. They were Food Network foodies who needed fresh herbs and cilantro whenever they wanted. The only thing these people had in common was that they ate daily.

So instead of frustrating ourselves by creating an ad that tried to appeal to everybody, and glanced off the mark, we needed a campaign that matched the messages of each audience to a media location where they resided. We had four clear purchasers: moms, home chefs, avid gardeners, and what we'll lump together as floral decorators. Thank goodness there were identifiable media outlets for each.

We created a series of four spots, all of which started with the question, "What are you going to grow today?" A question borrowed from our admiration of the "Got Milk?" campaign. Each spot starred a dramatized member of the specific group describing his or her problem with his or her categorical answer to the question. The gardener grew fresh, full tomatoes in December. The floral lover had fresh flowers in a living display all year long. The mom grew closer to her family by offering fresh meals enhanced easily with herbs. Finally, the pampered chef consumer "grew a party" anytime, with fresh tomatoes and basil, while being the envy of his or her friends. All of the spots drove either an online purchase, a call for a catalogue, or a discount coupon good at particular retailers where the product was sold. The spots all met with success, and we were able to tie all four executions together into a five-minute long form that was placed on certain cable networks that had that time available. The net effect of placing these spots in the correct media was to increase their individual performances as they spoke directly to a specific audience, with an offer that was tailor made to each one of these consumer segments. The messaging became different in each spot, tweaked to the order of value for purchase preference. The best part for the clients was that the direct response nature of the offers put them in the discounted space of media, to get more bang for the buck while achieving customer sales, inquiries, and data. Again, why doesn't everybody do this?

The Intersection of the Internet

The "next big thing" for our industry is still in the process of being discovered, as you read this. There are three technological scrambles that are happening at once, and they are sure to revolutionize the entire landscape of how the world markets products. One starts in the streets of Tokyo; the second is behind the unseen wall of the Internet; the third is in your living room.

Mobile marketing is being talked a lot about in the marketing backrooms of every company. Your cell phone has changed your identity. Like it or not, it is an electronic leash; but it's also a portal to efficiency, like no other device before it. Just as police and search-and-rescue teams rely on cell phones to find hikers when they are lost in the wilderness, direct markets have already begun to search for you, the consumer, as you roam the streets of your hometown. The Japanese have already figured this out; and, in America, we're on our way.

The Japanese consumer today is already entirely adapted to the true mobile marketing experience. As they walk through Tokyo, average consumers can rely on their phones to track their exact distance and proximity to particular retailers. They can be barraged with a variety of direct response offers, coupons, and instructions from vendors offering incentives to purchase and do business.

Imagine how you will feel when you are within a hundred yards of Starbucks, and Howard Schultz sends you a personal invitation to stop in now and get a dollar off your favorite Grande vanilla latte. The person walking next to you gets hit up for $2 off a bagel and soy cappuccino. These will not be random offers; they will be the items you have shown statistically to favor. Ten years ago that would have seemed if not far-fetched, certainly futuristic. Today, it is not.

The mobile marketing world is not at all far away from this technology; it just needs one thing: audience participation. Who knows? By the time you read this, it may already be routine. The point is, not some, *all* of our clients are fully prepared to engage in this model as soon as there is acceptance. Service companies like Yelp are already digging deep roots for your

mobile retail business, and as soon as the American corporation is convinced that there is more attraction than repulsion
to this idea, you will see it blossom here.

Meanwhile, the geeks are busy, very busy. They are moving
to track your consumer identity, and they have a big head start.
In the 1990s, a company called Catalina Marketing, based in
St. Petersburg, Florida, exploded onto the retail stage with an
advancement that you participate in almost daily. Go to the
grocery store, the hardware store, the movie theater or the big-
box retailer, and you might very well be "touched" by Catalina
and companies like it. What these marketing companies do is
track consumer data precisely. Do you ever turn over your grocery receipt? Do you see coupons? That's most likely Catalina.
What the firm is doing is tracking the scan data from your purchases, and holding it. The coupons Catalina issues are from
corporations that want your business. Buy baby food, and you'll
see coupons on the back for diapers. Buy beer, and you may get
an offer from a potato chip or snack food manufacturer.

Why do retailers participate? The system costs them nothing. They have the opportunity to entice you back, to get
that next promotional deal. Catalina calls it *loyalty marketing*.
There's nothing a retailer needs more than your loyalty. At
the end of the day, what's the business about? Data. Consumer
companies want the data on what you buy for a variety of reasons, most importantly: increasing market share of product,
widening their corporate footprint on shelves, and improving
brand value.

As direct marketers we know that nothing is more important than your data. If we know where you shop, how you shop,
and what you shop for, we know where to find you. At Cesari
Direct, we rely on outside intelligence to license us tools to
help find you today through media, and get our USP in front
of you, both on television and the web. As the world scrambles
to start collecting and intersecting the data points, you can

bet our industry will move far beyond television and into your mobile devices, and more.

The third horizon that we are all attempting to look beyond is back in your home, with broadband digital cable. Right now, most of us go home and either work off a hard-wired PC or a wireless laptop. We really use our television as a separate appliance, one we mostly just view. I realized this was going to change the day I got an Apple TV. For those who have not experienced a Roku box or Apple TV, what you get as a consumer is limited access to the web through your 42-inch plasma screen. Order a movie for direct download through your cable system and you'll begin to understand. I fully enjoy watching YouTube in my family room. For the past three years, at the Consumer Electronics Show in Las Vegas, almost every cable company has introduced the advent of television Internet access.

If you are under 40 years old, you'll say, "So what?" I'm over 40, so I had to figure it out. What television Internet means is that a day is coming very soon when every web site in the world will no longer be a web site; it will be a worldwide on-demand broadcast network. "So what?" you say again. At the moment, there is no cost to broadcast and no version of the FTC policing the web. Let that sink in for a moment. Television advertising is about to change, forever.

If you own a URL, you can effectively drive traffic to a terrific global television network, virtually for free. You will not be a slave to programming schedules, forced placement of ads, or time-limit constraints. Programming, all programming, will be selected by the viewer. Including the commercials.

Consumers will soon have the chance to click through and order directly off their television sets with their remote controls. A direct television offer will be just that, truly direct—point-and-click and charge to your cable bill or credit card you set up to bill to. Imagine every television program and ad with an available cursor that enables you to point and click to purchase.

CHAPTER
12

Free Advertising?

The challenge advertising has always presented, in any form, including direct response, is how to pay the least to get the most valuable leads. Our DNA as advertisers has always been to try and get our message, our product, and our offer in front of you the viewer. The assumption is that we have to pay to sneak in front of you and hopefully reward you with something that gets your attention. What if that changed?

Assume you know nothing. Why do I watch the Super Bowl? Yes, I love pro football, but half the reason I watch the Super Bowl is that I love advertising. I can't wait to see the creativity of the guys and gals behind the E*TRADE talking babies, Budweiser, or FedEx. I like advertising; and so do you. The traditional assumption is that the viewer is avoiding advertising, avoiding messaging, and avoiding being sold to; but as we said in the beginning, that's just not true. We like advertising that is about us, that tells us about our lives, specifically, and how we can look better, feel better, and live better. The new challenge is about to become how to be self-selected by viewers to be on their "favorites" list for media.

The collision of the new technologies is going to allow for something that is almost unbelievable, free advertising—truly free advertising, or at the very least advertising that is self-sustaining direct response. Think about your e-mail. Buy a plane ticket, rent a car, or visit an online retailer and you get e-mail direct response offers from those companies. Much of it you do not delete or block because you want it. I want to know about the next new car, or the online closeouts from Eddie Bauer and Williams-Sonoma. You have yours.

Now take that paradigm and lay it on top of your electronic world. Come home and only see the TV programs you want, when you want. The ads are all about your interests, and the media is all about you. We already have brands of news that report the world the way we prefer to see it. That world is about to change.

We often joke at our company that the definition of technology is the following: Technology is the sum of the collective human experience that endeavors to ensure we have no more collective human experience. You will soon be able to create the "marketing bubble" that you will live in. What will be the value of customer acquisition that day? Staggering.

We have always lived in a world where the idea of "push marketing" was the norm. Advertisers currently pay a premium to push concepts in front of you. Moving forward, it will become primarily "pull." You will only seek advertising that addresses the categories and products that you want. Google is the new norm. You want something, you seek it, sort it, and get it. It's all about the consumer. Pull marketing is the new norm. Get used to it, and learn how to take advantage of it.

Is My Idea Direct-Response Worthy?

This is one of the most common questions we get. Most likely, if it is not today, it may be soon. But living in the present, how do we decide when we talk to an inventor or a corporation whether direct response offers an answer for your marketing plan? We start with two main questions:

- First, do you have a USP? Have you discovered something that is truly unique, that's different from the art prior to it? Can it be easily explained or demonstrated? If the answer is yes, you are halfway there.

- Second, is there a media channel that draws an audience that will support sales of your product? Is it a "pet product?" Maybe it can find success on Animal Planet? Is it a product that ends bad doggie breath after he or she eats? You might have something. Is it a beauty accessory for iguanas? Today, there's no media channel to support that; but someday there may be a media outlet that specializes in content for reptile owners. If your product can be quantified to a degree that proves there is an audience that is defined by a media outlet, you have taken a big step in the right direction.

Those are the first two factors we look at when we review a product: *USP* and *audience*. If you are an inventor or a writer of intellectual property content and answered yes to both of these questions, then you are probably ready to start looking more seriously at DR.

Next, we ask a battery of questions, starting with potential audience size. Since there are just a few of us, and our time is finite, we look for a few more things than the two just described. We tend to represent products that we believe can be placed in a large demographic or an aggregate of consumer segments, which we can justify as adding up to a large aggregate. If you looked at that number as 30 to 80 percent of the general populous, you'd probably make it over that hurdle as well. The vast majority of successful products really require these kinds of numbers—though there *are* exceptions to this rule of thumb (for a valid example, see the box below).

 Walk-in Tubs

To understand how what might seem a niche market can work well in DR, consider the case of Premier Care in Bathing. Premier is in the business of selling a high-end, walk-in bathtub that serves seniors with mobility issues.

(continued)

(*continued*)

That's a fairly narrow product category with a very specific consumer. Primarily, the audience is either seniors who want to stay in their homes as long as they can, or their adult children who want to keep Mom or Dad comfortable and safe in their homes. The economic driver for this category is huge, when you look at the costs of in-home nursing assistance or moving into assisted living.

The product fills a clear need—a practical need, an emotional need, and a financial need. The audience for the product is, however, statistically small—the home does not need this product today—but the media for this consumer is highly targetable, and thus very successful. Premier Care in Bathing has done very well utilizing direct response television and the web as lead generators for potential customers who eventually buy. The lower cost of DR ad placement ensures that the company can maximize its exposure while recruiting prospects that are in the market for this $10,000-plus product.

The financial mechanics make this product the exception. It is a very small audience, but a high-ticket item. Perhaps your product has a unique aspect to its business model, as well.

The reason we look for numbers that large is our intense interest in creating brands. Remember, brand is something that can occupy consumer space and disrupt sales of existing products, to "build in" an exit strategy for our clients. We are very aggressive in the brand category, as the divergent segmentation of markets will require it for consumer goods today, and even more so in the future.

The next hurdle is cost of goods (COGs). Pragmatic business decisions about DR always have to consider the available dollars for marketing when we succeed. If you have a product that costs $20 to build, and can capture a retail of only $40, you are out of the direct response business before you start. We prefer to see companies and entrepreneurs come to the table with a 4- or 5-to-1 margin. That means if your product costs $8 to $10 to manufacture, you need to be confident that you can make a case to the consumer that it justifies a retail of about $40. That equation stays pretty true until you get to over $100 in cost of goods, and then the ratio of 3-to-1 tends to hold true.

Why Are the COGs So Important?

Properly controlling cost of goods is essential in any form of business. Almost all businesses have operating costs that include office rent, human resources, utilities, equipment, vendor costs, cost of goods, taxes, and marketing. As the scale and volume of a business grow, you need to have space to cover expenses as they shift. In direct marketing, as you begin to build brand value and increase exposure, you increase demand. As demand grows, the opportunity to open up retail distribution networks becomes paramount. Even though your sales volume may be increasing, and you are profitable, don't rush out and buy that cigarette boat and Ferrari! Not quite yet.

Retailers will want your product because they see it on television; they know the power of direct response. They know that, frequently, for every one unit sold on television there may be the opportunity to sell four, five, or six at retail. When they begin to call, you are going to need available resources to ramp up inventory while still spending media dollars. It is very common for a product to do very well on TV then release onto retail shelves and experience a decline in direct sales through television and the web. That does not mean you turn off your direct response. In fact, most often, you turn it up, because you are driving a great deal of retail volume.

Remember, when you sell inventory to the retailer, you are only getting a portion of the price for which you sold it to direct customers. A product with a $20 COGs might sell for $40 on TV, but the retailer will probably only pay $20. If you were at a 2-to-1 ratio, you'd be toast. The good news is the retailer will order entire pallets of product, which increases your efficiencies. The huge decrease you experience in gross dollars per unit you will more than make up for in volume of units sold. This is why cost of goods is so important: Proper margin insulates your operating costs and profit model down the road.

This becomes really clear when you look at the basic numbers for starting a direct response campaign. Let's assume you have a product that costs $10 to produce and get into a distribution warehouse, and that you are selling it for $39.95, plus shipping and processing. The basic elements of a direct response campaign include a telesales company to answer your calls, a fulfillment warehouse to ship orders, the shipping service itself, and cost of media. Here are some round numbers for argument's sake.

Product	COGs	Telesales	Fulfillment	S&P	Media	Total	Retail
1 unit	$10	$2	$2	$3	$10	$27	$39.95 + $4.95 S&P Total: $44.90

It costs you $27 to completely execute an order, for which you are charging the consumer $44.90. You have paid your COGs and your vendors ($27). Congratulations! You have $17.90 profit per unit to pay for any core operational business costs and to reimburse your start-up costs. You are in business.

When you move to wholesaling units into retail, the model shifts and you eliminate some costs, but your cash collected drops, as shown here.

Product	COGs	Telesales	Fulfillment	S&P	Media	Total	Wholesale
1 unit	$10	0	0	0	0	$10	$20

Now, in the retail segment of your business you've collected $20 per unit, and your COGs are only $10. You're hopefully selling five times more units, so your gross cash increases. But, remember, your retailers are still going to want to see you supporting that product with media, which means you need to find a way to stay on TV profitably and drive the brand. The answer is to broaden the brand with a new product, which changes the television/web offer, and create a new DR ad that includes this new SKU that retail doesn't carry. You'll subsidize the cost of advertising with the sales you make and have a powerful engine to drive existing retail. This is not an idea. This is not a guess. This is a strategy we have proved to ourselves over and over. It makes *everybody* buy, now!

This is exactly what we did with OxiClean, the George Foreman Grill, and Space Bags. More items and richer television offers that motivate the early adopters to keep buying from television. Certainly, you can maintain the price of the offer; in fact, more times than not, the TV offer is far more expensive than any retail offer, but it is jam-packed with SKUs that present great value to the consumer. This strategy keeps you fresh, keeps you on TV, and pushes retail sales to the "tactile" group of consumers who absolutely refuse to buy anything without touching it first. Yes, you give up a significant amount of profit on the direct response sales. So what? You are making money hand over fist on retail and have cracked the code of Walmart, Target, Federated, Home Depot, and the rest.

George Foreman Grills became larger and more expensive with each show, offering more bells and whistles. OxiClean product bundles became larger, and even broadened into the company's other products like KABOOM and Orange Clean. Space Bag offers featured more, and more different-sized, bags for travel, closet storage, garment, and even comforter-sized bags.

Having a product with an "intelligent" cost of goods was part of the necessary alchemy of a perfect brand-building exercise, one that resulted in millions of dollars of sales for each of these products and created a hugely successful exit strategy for the founders, paying off in either tens to hundreds of millions of dollars in each case. That's fun to participate in—and, yes, you can do it. The people behind each one of these brands were smart, caring, and hard-working. We have to imagine that if you purchased this book, so are you.

There is no magic to launching a successful brand. The secrets are all here. Actually, as you can see, they are not really secrets. It's more a path. Follow the path and you will get the results. It really is that simple. If it wasn't, we wouldn't be able to replicate it over and over for so many years and apply the method to so many different product and service categories. There is nothing particularly unique about the people who are successful in this industry. We've met nice people, not so nice people, smart people, and some not so smart. In fact, sometimes it can be easier for the not-so-smart because they *know* they don't know. If you assume you know nothing, and are willing to move forward with humility, you almost can't help but succeed.

Long Form or Short Form? That Is the Question

This is an interesting topic, in that the answer, at first blush, seems to most people to be financially driven. They think all short-form spots are for $19.95 or $9.95 products. Certainly the first ones that come to mind are, since, historically, that was the case in the industry. The Veg-O-Matic, Pocket Fisherman, and ShamWow proved that that price point can be a driver for some products. The answer is not so simple today.

If you are an inventor and have an item that you would classify as a gadget, *and* your cost of goods is around $2 to $3, *and* 80 percent of Americans truly need and can use your product daily, *and* it's a highly demonstrable product that solves a common problem *and* has powerful before-and-after examples, then, yes, you are probably living in a short-form world. That type of product represents only a small segment of the short-form time being purchased today.

Today, the vast majority of short-form time is being gobbled up by advertisers that use the format to drive you to the Internet. They are looking to convert a much higher-ticket or consumable item that consumers will return for, like a service or even a pharmaceutical. Sure, there are plenty of gardening products, pet products, and sunglasses to get your $9.95 business, but they are the fringe of overall spending. The real dollars are starting to flow through agencies like ours that are buying for traditional brands or new DR brands that have been built in the space. eHarmony, FreeCreditReport.com, E*TRADE, and Overstock.com are all brands that have generated $100 million or far more in annual revenue, based solely on direct response.

Price no longer is the driver of short-form direct response, thanks to the web. A better indicator is whether your "story" can be told effectively in the 2-minute, 1-minute, and 30-second formats. Can you make it enticing for me to visit your URL to learn more? Tantalizing the viewer with an offer is a primary strategy. eHarmony offers free views of actual profiles of potential matches, and free communication with them, for limited periods of time. You do, however, have to give a substantial amount of data to the site before you can even discover the actual cost of joining, including name, birth date, and home and e-mail addresses. Once the company has your credit card number, it knows exactly who you are! Our increased comfort with giving our personal information over the web is making Internet business a lion in the direct response jungle.

Long form is the traditional "infomercial," our bread and butter for the first decade in the business. And long-form shows and media still account for a substantial portion of our volume, primarily because we were in the industry early and created our own "style" of informed learning that sells. We have traditionally succeeded with shows that have a very pragmatic and sincere feel to them, and our pitch is typically very matter-of-fact and direct.

How long does it take for you to explain your product or service to a friend before you see that lightbulb go off in his or her mind? If it takes more than 45 seconds, you probably need a long-form program. Is your product a device that retails for more than $40 and is a new technology nobody has seen before? It probably needs a long form. This is why you see so many pieces of exercise equipment, home improvement and garden products, and intellectual property products start in long form. You need the time to explain the USP, and consumers need the time to see the device function and hear from the experts who endorse it or invented it. There's just too much ground to cover in 60 seconds. There are many examples of companies that have launched with a long-form show then eventually migrated to short form. We have done it with almost every long form we created.

Anatomy of an Infomercial

You may have seen many long-form shows, and you certainly will relate to the following parts and pieces. We include them here so that when you are writing your own, or hiring someone to do that for you, you clearly understand the basics and have some of the lingo down. There are no hard-and-fast rules here—without question, there are infomercials that have deviated from this formulaic observation and succeeded. There are shows that include pieces outside the formula that are brilliant, as well. This discussion is to just get you started.

Note that the times given here for the basic parts and pieces of the infomercial formula are approximations.

- *Opening Disclaimer (5 seconds; required)*: The FCC requires all long-form shows to reveal that they are paid programming. You must state this with both an audio voice-over and graphic stating the legal name of the business entity that is purchasing the airtime.
- *The Tease (1 to 3 minutes)*: The tease serves to set up the problem you are going to address and solve with your new product. Teases often start with the emotional or personal "pain points" that "set the table" for the show. This is where you typically ask the questions directly to the consumer that identify and engage them, for example:
  - "Are you seeing more lines and wrinkles around your eyes every morning?"
  - "Are you self-conscious wearing a swimsuit in public?"
  - "Does your car look, feel, and smell showroom-new?"

All simple questions that evoke a visceral response from the consumer, questions for which you actually control the answer and the response. After all, who *isn't* self-conscious in a swimsuit?

You will use some time in the tease to share your innovation, describe the benefit(s), and briefly state your unique selling proposition. Often, a tease will include small sound-bite testimonials, animations, and the juiciest visual elements that preview what the viewer will be seeing. Typically, you will address the voice of the skeptics, as well, inviting them to "see for themselves" the independent evidence. A great tease will end by delivering an intense sense of engagement and anticipation that will transition effortlessly into the main body of the show. Your goal is to engage the viewers so they simply get swept away in the stream and end up watching the show compulsively.

- *Show Body:* Typically, the show body comprises three acts separated by "calls to action," or CTAs. We frequently have three acts that are approximately eight minutes, six minutes, and three minutes, in descending length, and separated by two CTAs (described later in the chapter). The show body can be in many formats.

The following sections describe a few of the industry show body standards.

Show Styles or Formats

The News Talk Show or Televised Radio Talk Show

This is probably the number-one style of show used by entrepreneurs, due to its low cost to produce and simple discussion format. Typically, a host interviews an expert guest or inventor to discuss a book, a supplement, or a collection of intellectual property that has been developed. The topics often cover making money, weight loss, and health issues.

The Daytime Women's Talk Show
Formulated to look and feel like some form of daytime chat show, this format may have two to eight women sitting around a living room set discussing a product. Beauty products seem to reign in this arena. The participants are often the "inventor" of the product, a celebrity or two, a host, and "real women," who provide the endorsement and testimonial evidence. This is the format that Guthy-Renker has mastered admirably.

The Demonstration Show
This format typically has an expert pitchman walking through a set demonstrating a new product. He or she shows a variety of applications and usages, illustrating ease of use, incredible effects, and all the features and benefits. Sometimes a studio audience is incorporated. This common show style lends itself to kitchen products, housewares, hardware products, beds, fitness products, and auto products. The demonstration show is one of our favorite long-form styles because it can be executed with a high degree of direct pragmatic sincerity.

The Storymercial
Although on occasion I have seen the storymercial used with success, the risk of this type of marketing is far too great for me, personally, to bite on as a marketer. The conceit of a storymercial is that it appears as a dramatic program with fictional characters that are experiencing a problem in life that the product solves. Perhaps there was a moment in time when this was the ideal way to come to market, but today's prevalence of reality television programming makes a dramatized long form a risky proposition.

We have never attempted a storymercial, and I do not recommend this format for long form. Having said that, the concept of the dramatized problem-and-solution model has proven to work in the short-form space for many, many companies, including ours, and I would highly recommend this kind of dramatization for short form. The trick is to make the story feel and appear real. Currently, the campaign that best exemplifies the short-form dramatization, in my mind, is the eHarmony campaign. All the actors and actresses in it look like legitimate couples that have been matched by eHarmony. It is so well executed that the viewer never considers that the stories are manufactured.

The Host Tour

This type of show may take place in a studio, a home, or outdoors, live, and is typically chosen to introduce a new or complex technology with many components. A single host walks viewers through the product and shows them its benefits and features, in detail. The host "throws" to outside segments that help validate the multifaceted product. Occasionally, the host may appear with subjects in a studio, to explain essential components, or with a scientist and the founders to validate the product. A studio audience is rare with this format, but an option.

These shows work well for complex products and new technologies. Many of this type of show are being used to roll out web- and health-based products, where the host appears in a "virtual world' and interacts with a variety of animated and graphic components. The budgets on shows like these can be very affordable, and they have a dramatically high production value when executed properly.

This is a style of program we routinely turn to for its direct, compelling, informative approach and proven sales record.

The Reality Approach

This emerging new prince of infomercials will no doubt become king, particularly as established brands with identifiable USPs move into direct response. The reality infomercial relies on consumer-generated reviews and usage of products and services. Consumer self-shot video is the rising sun in advertising. It is the filmed equivalent of an Epinions.com or Amazon.com review. Our client Beachbody has tapped this over and over in the past three years, with P90X and its new exercise smash Insanity.

A great way to launch a new idea is to let people try it, then submit unadulterated video. The reality style often still has a host, to tie the information together, but in a much lighter balance than a host-driven show. Recently Activia, a Danone brand, grabbed this element in short form. In the campaign, Jamie Lee Curtis hosts "real-user"-submitted video from consumers talking about their improved "dietary tract" and "regular" benefits achieved thanks to the product. The spots are currently run in traditional media, but they could easily reach even more women with a direct response media plan, as the creative is a web driver for couponing and video submission.

■ ■ ■

Again, these are just some of the choices in show body styles that are out there.

Long-Form Elements

The CTA—Call to Action

All long forms have a two- to five-minute segment that appears several times in the show, usually twice, sometimes three times; this is the all-important *call to action*. The CTA is what we often consider to be the single most important element of a show, as it can absolutely make or break your entire creative.

In your CTA you have a very short time to, again, set up the problem for the consumer and make it real and "painful." This places them in a state of discomfort, which you will immediately remedy with your product and its USP. More importantly, this will be your chance to build a solid value proposition. You might refer to existing technologies that don't quite cut the mustard, for one reason or another. You might explain the costs and aggravation; perhaps even the embarrassment of seeking a "professional" solution.

Then you need to get to the second most important part of your marketing plan, after the explanation of your USP: the offer. Your offer must feel like a relief to the consumers. You cannot disappoint them! They want and deserve a favorable offering that rewards them for watching and limits their financial barrier to entry. Give them an included premium, something that you would want but not necessarily buy for yourself. A "gift for purchase" the consumer keeps, even if he or she returns the product, increases confidence. Offer to pay for shipping if you can. This is not the same as "free shipping" in consumers' minds. The normal assumption is that you are screwing them on shipping, so by offering to pay the shipping on their behalf makes them conscious that there is, in fact, a cost to shipping and that you are picking it up. This makes you a nicer company. Figuring this out was the key that unlocked the Amazon.com marketing beast. It truly was the game-changer for the company. (Living in Seattle, we get good inside scoops from time to time!) Dropping a payment has become expected by the consumer, as well. If you plan on selling for three payments of $39.95, start out at four. And back everything you sell with at least a 30-day guarantee. Why? Because it is so widely practiced and accepted that if you do not, you should not expect to sell a single unit.

Your CTA will end with a 20- to 30-second *tag*, which is the offer read out loud in brief, along with the 1-800 number and web site. The tag is read individually to every station dub that is sent out, and each version typically has a unique 1-800 phone number, for the purpose of tracking call volume and sales attributable to an airing.

Testimonials

Testimonials from real-world participants are essential. You should expect to have 4 to 10 sprinkled throughout your show, with sound bites to boot in the tease and CTA. Earlier we discussed the P90X and the power of its reality testimonials. As true as that holds, it does not mean that all of your testimonials need be photographed in a self-shot style. Testimonials should always be cultivated from real user groups; the users should never be paid, and they should never be actors. Don't cut corners.

How do you get testimonials for a new product? Be patient. Create a small web site, or advertise your product on a small scale, and let people purchase it. When they do, collect their data and give them about four weeks before you follow up with a customer service call, to inquire about your product's performance. Our new and favorite place to find actual consumers is the web. We often look at web reviews and call consumers who have submitted letters of praise to ask if they are willing to share their testimonies on camera. It is unethical to solicit testimonials with payment, gifts, trips, or inducements. For entrepreneurial projects, however, long after the show has rolled out, we have sent thank-you notes, sometimes with a gift card or second product. Again, the testimonial participant must not be aware of this, even if it is your intention. No promises for endorsements!

If a product requires long-term usage, such as a weight-loss product, it is perfectly acceptable to monitor participants' progress; but, again, the experience they are having must duplicate the consumer experience. No special coaching; they must purchase the product and use it as any "normal" participant does. This is not legal advice, just good advice.

Professional Endorsements

Yes, they matter. Doctors, physical therapists, construction managers, chefs, beauty professionals, and the like have appeared in every successful infomercial over the past 25 years.

Experts are essential; they let the viewer know that someone with actual experience and credibility says you are telling the truth. Be aware that if you have paid a professional for his or her time, you must divulge it in the form of a disclaimer that is clearly visible under his or her image. And if the professional is materially connected to the company, you must display that information prominently, as well.

Finally, all professionals giving testimonials should sign a usage waiver that clearly states they are giving you their testimonies in its full and truthful context. Always edit testimonials to reflect the true context. A good product will always have people who want to support it and are willing to appear on television.

Animation

At Cesari Direct, we have learned through the use of focus groups and dial testing, (which allows a second by second analysis of a commercial), that animation is probably the single most compelling sales tool you have in your arsenal to close a consumer. Do not underestimate animation, and learn how to use it as much and as frequently as possible. Here's what we think we know about it:

Think about the first time you came in contact with animation in America; it was during your childhood. We all watched and loved cartoons, as far back as *Steamboat Willie* in our grandparents' day. I know we grew up with Hanna-Barbera Cartoons, and Looney Tunes, and the like. The thing about cartoons is that they show the truly impossible, yet come across as believable— or at the very least, allow us to suspend disbelief—like nothing else. The advent of video games has only increased the effect for younger generations. Image is reality to many people.

Animation allows you to show consumers the ins and outs of your product in a way they could never experience it in the real world. It provides the "incredible journey" into the inner workings and "facts" of your product. The irony of animation is that it is literally the most simplified and manufactured element of any show. Ironically, consumers often see it as the opposite. Now, I am not suggesting that you manufacture false information in the course of executing a good animation, only that you take full advantage of the medium.

In a good show about an air purification product, for example, at some point you will see the air purifier in an animation. You will "shrink down" to the microscopic world and take a tour that feels like a cross between Mr. Toad's Wild Ride and Space Mountain at Disneyland. Animation can take the unbelievable and put it right in the consumer's mind.

Here's a current example of animation's power over the consumer. In our BackJoy campaign, we are selling a pain-relieving orthotic for the back, which you sit on. There are two inherent problems with this product from a demonstration angle. First, when you sit on the product, it disappears. Second, the structural change effected by a back orthotic happens primarily inside the human body. You simply cannot easily see what the product does if you don't know what to look for. We overcame that problem with an animation.

Before the host demonstrates the usage of the product for the first time at the beginning of the show, he walks the viewer through an explanation via animation. Viewers get to see a before-and-after of the device, complete with its external and internal effects on the human body. When we come out of the animation, viewers see the product used in the real world for the first time, and because the expectation and learning is already planted in their minds, they can clearly see the effect.

Show Outline

We like to tell people that the structure of an infomercial is like the structure of a good speech or presentation: tell your audience what you are going to say, say it, and then tell them what you said.

In summary, if you were to have a basic generic map for a show flow of a long-form infomercial it would look something like this.

TEASE: (2 minutes) Setup and explanation of USP

ACT ONE

Host (2 minutes): Sets up problem, reveals solution/USP (possible demo)

Animation (1 minute): Host voice, announcer voice, or expert voice

Host (1 minute): Deeper info (possible demo)

Testimonial (2 minutes)

Expert Testimonial (1 minute)

Host Throw to CTA 1 (30 seconds)

CTA 1 (2–5 minutes): Problem/solution—value build→ offer→tag

ACT TWO

Host (2 minutes): Resets problem and solution USP (possible demo)

Expert (or founder) Testimonial (1 minute)

Testimonial (1 minute)

Host (demo)

Host Throw to CTA 2

CTA 2 (2–5 minutes) Problem/solution—value build→ offer→tag

ACT THREE

Host (2 minutes): Possible demo

Recap of offer by host, with urge to call

Short CTA or tag, with consumer testimonials

That's all the parts and pieces of a basic infomercial. It looks fairly simple and easy to create, but accept this fair warning: This is a little like me telling you the parts and pieces of an airplane. There's no guarantee that because you can identify them you'll be able to build one in your garage that will fly! Remember, we started our careers in direct response advertising when the market was a whole lot more forgiving. Today's consumer is looking at your program like a critical producer. Flaws and moments of phoniness will stand out like a sore thumb.

CHAPTER
14

Offer Is King

W e have been around this industry since the beginning; we know just about everybody. Internally, it is a surprisingly friendly industry where most of the players know each other, golf together at industry events, and sit elbow to elbow at dinners a few times a year. We applaud success for one another, because sooner or later everyone gets to hit one out of the park. In almost every senior creative person's office, somewhere there will be a plaque a sign or a moniker of some sort that reads, "Offer Is King."

Offer is the single most malleable driver of calls and sales volume you will have at your disposal when you create a DRTV commercial. You must be prepared to have a number of offers to test. If you are a corporate marketing person, if you are an inventor, do this:

Get out your scissors and cut out the sentence shown here in boldface and all caps. Then, just like you would the slip of paper from a fortune cookie, tape it to your computer monitor. You will read it and, initially, have resistance; but you must, *must* believe us when we say this:

WHEN YOU TEST A LONG-FORM SHOW, ALWAYS MAKE THE MOST CONSUMER-FRIENDLY OFFER YOU CAN IN YOUR FIRST TEST.

Read it again.

One more time.

You will always be tempted to test first an offer that makes you the most money up front. That temptation is driven by ego, an ego that tells you, "If I have made a great show, people will beat a path to my door and cough up the full cash price, *now*! That's, frankly, not smart, and it's not accurate. We create many shows. In fact, I'd say that, at times, we've specialized in high-ticket products and services. Yet we've never had a show work on that high-ticket price. A payment plan is always required. Then, once the phone rings, about 15 percent of your total orders will convert to a single payment at the full price. Coincidentally, this is statistically a good approximation of the sample audience that is the wealthiest of consumers.

Having the most consumer-friendly offer allows you to test the creative of the show. A successful test will give the entire marketing team an emotional lift and let you know that you have proof of concept on a scalable rate. Once you have done that, go back and fine-tune the financial mechanics to optimize your business model with further offer testing that improves your profit margin.

Let me tell a quick story to explain where I learned this lesson. We worked with a company that manufactured a product in the exercise category. It was a machine. The company had worked very hard to get the COGs down to about $70. Everyone agreed they just could not afford to be in business unless the device sold for at least $200.

We created a show with photography that was awesome, featuring attractive, fit models. The product looked great, substantial, and valuable. It was tested at three payments of $79, plus shipping. It failed to make breakeven. The decision was to go back out at six payments of $39 to account for what seemed to be a first-payment barrier to entry. The second test performed worse. We were all depressed, defeated, and demoralized. Then one of our lower-level folks—we are pretty sure it was an art department assistant—said, "I just don't get it; this thing looks as good as a Bowflex or a Soloflex, and those cost about 800 to 1,000 bucks."

Assume you know nothing!

The next test was for a trial payment of $14.95 for the first 30 days. The call center used the increased call volume this generated and discovered that the device would easily support the volume to roll out a campaign at $400. The next week we tested $500, then $600, then $700, and finally $800. Seven hundred settled in as the winner. Here, the client had developed a marketing argument that looked and felt so good that when arriving at the price of $200, it caused a huge disconnect for the consumer. To consumers, it was actually a letdown. They believed that at the low price the quality and workmanship had to be garbage. It wasn't. It was very good quality in a design that happened to be very cost-effective to build.

Everybody on the project would have given up on this product had we not reacted to that assistant's visceral response from looking at the device. The lesson here is: Get the phone to ring using an offer that gives you consumers to interact with, then test, test, test.

Now, go back and cut out that bold sentence and stick it on your computer. After all, you've already read the page!

Why Is Everything Priced at $19.95 and $39.95?

It seems that every infomercial offer is priced the same: Either it's $19.95 for short form or $39.95 for long form. This is actually not true, but we understand it sure feels that way.

The Infomercial Monitoring Service, Inc. (IMS), along with Jordan Whitney, keeps tabs on the infomercial industry as a whole. Would you be surprised to find out that of the top 20 short-form spots airing in America the week of October 4, 2010, only one was priced $19.95. It's true. The number-one most common short-form offer has become a driver to a web site that converts to purchase of a product or service. In second place is the typical widget offer at $9.95. This offer often "doubles" the unit volume for a second S&P, representing a small 20 percent of the top 20. After that, there are a variety of offers that start at a free trial and move up to $14.95 paid trials, for fitness equipment that actually costs hundreds. The introduction of so many offers at $19.95 and $39.95, and the many years of dominance of these price points, is probably the mechanism that cements it in our minds. But is there "something" to these numbers? We believe there is.

Our hours and hours spent in focus groups and dial testing groups have been insightful for us in many ways. Price can be a very difficult thing to quantify and get right in the context of a group. We frankly do not trust what consumers say in a focus group about specific price points, as the conversation usually digresses to a point where the group agrees that they should be offered to try every product in the world for free. That is not how they behave in the real world, however; consumers routinely pay real money for products. What is insightful is not *what* they think but *how* they think.

Categorically, we feel confident in reporting that consumers think in incremental dollar values—the first being $20 bills. Consumers seem to readily think about the amount of money they are spending in increments of twenties—$19.95, $39.95, $59.95, $79.95. These are the prices that are powerful in direct response. We are certainly aware that other prices work, but are talking in broad brushstrokes here.

Somewhere in the middle of 2004, we were involved in a comfort product, a pillow that we tested at $29.95, $39.95, $49.95, and $59.95. In identical versions of the show we were simply testing call volume and pricing. The call volume for the $29 version and $39 version was identical. The call volume for the $49 version and the $59 version was lower than the cheaper versions, but, again, identical to each other. The consumer saw no difference between $29 and $39, nor between $49 and $59—$20 increments.

Above and beyond the total price of $100, and up to $500, consumers typically are willing to see payment schemes that are also in $20 increments, from $19.95 to $39.95 to $59.95, and finally, $79.95 for the most expensive products.

Direct marketers do not sell widgets and devices exclusively. As you've seen by now, our industry represents computers, cars, vacations, home remodeling, health clubs, construction products, pools, roofs, and a whole realm of high-end goods. There are price points for products that far exceed $1,000, and the payment schemes for those products tend to follow the more accepted ones that are industry-specific. The offer expressed for these types of goods is the all-important DVD. Don't miss the chance to generate a clean, solid lead, plus get the opportunity to send consumers a 70¢ brochure in the form of a DVD as you capture their data. You'll even get to repurpose all that great infomercial content that you were forced to leave on the editing bay floor!

If you have a consumer product that costs over $10,000, has an audience that you can identify in a media channel, and are not using direct response to find new business, you are missing sales. That's an absolute fact.

How Do Long Form and Short Form Work Together?

Operating under the assumption that you have a product that is complex enough to require a long-form show, to build awareness and sales to fund your growth, your long-form launch will also help identify the new category you want to establish. Getting the business up and functioning with actual sales and cash flow is the basic reason to start in long form for a breakthrough product that needs explanation.

So, assuming you have successfully done this, *when* do you move to short form, and do you run both at the same time? Now and yes! Here are the basic mechanics of how you will make that decision. Let's use the George Foreman Grill as the example.

When we introduced the grill, it was unheard of—remember, Salton had invented the "perfect taco meat maker." We had morphed it into the Lean Mean Fat-Reducing Grilling Machine. Heck, that almost takes 45 seconds to say. We *had* to have a long form to explain all its features and benefits and share all the dozens of types of meals you could make on it, thus proving you would use it every day. The first version of the product retailed at $59.95.

Once the grill was successful on television, retailers wanted it, so Salton initiated distribution, and we started making a show for the larger grill (it fit six burgers instead of four). The retailer loved this because the new machine still drove retail on the smaller device. The next step was to create a short form that sold the smaller device at $59.95 and still helped push retail. Now the question is, why did we push the small grill instead of the large? The answer is so obvious it's almost silly: *offer* and *time*.

The short-form, four-burger grill was established and understood by the consumer. The offer was easily expressible, at three payments of $19.95, which still worked in short form at the time. But the most important aspect was time—that is, available airtime.

Long-form airtime is only available when it's available. I'm sure you've noticed that this is, most frequently, early mornings, in the middle of the night, and weekend days. Generally, long forms run when the stations and networks have available holes in their programming schedules. This basic challenge does limit viewership, to a degree. Short-form time does not suffer this limitation.

Short-form direct response inventory is the saving grace of many television networks and the few individual broadcast stations that exist regionally. The short-form direct response advertiser offers financial flexibility to sell advertising slots that are not taken by brand advertisers, which purchase well in advance. The advantage of this is that it gives you the ability to place advertising within a "window" of programming on any network, even locally and regionally, to find your audience.

What's a "window"? It can be as long as two or three days or as short as three or four hours, depending on the individual network policy. An example would be purchasing a flight of media—let's say 20 total airings of a campaign divided by a 2-minute version, a 1-minute version, and a 30-second spot. Assume you have paid $2,000 for this bundle and put it on your local ABC affiliate in Phoenix, Arizona. As it plays out, the station runs the 2-minute 4 times, the 1-minute 12 times, and the 30-second 8 more times. You have paid for 20 airings; the station has thrown in some extra airings for free, which is common; so you end up with 24 airings at an average of $83 per airing. The station has placed it where it chooses; and you can bet if you negotiated for the 3:00 to 7:00 PM time slot, every day you ended up around some local news or evening magazine show. That means you were very close to the national ABC nightly news feed for that market, as well. That's good time.

Again, assuming these were accurate approximations for station rates during the George Foreman era, we would have needed to sell an average of two grills per airing in the general Phoenix area just to be above breakeven. That means you are essentially advertising for free to a new audience and in a time frame that further legitimizes the brand. As discussed earlier, for every unit we sell on television, multiple units are being sold at retail. That means your long form is busy building demand for yet another new product and offer.

This is the brand-building power of direct response in its truest form. As more short forms ran for George Forman Grills, and new products were added to the long-form schedule, we were able to create a rotation of marketing that forced retailers to expand their devoted shelf space for the grills, based on con-sumer demand. A typical George Forman retail customer might walk into Macy's and say, "Hey, I see you carry the George Forman Grill for $59.95, but I saw the large outdoor grill that cooks a dozen burgers on television this morning for $129. Do you have that?" Needless to say, Macy's called and wanted that one, too. This is the formula for building brand, getting shelf space, and creating a powerful exit strategy. This is a formula that you, as an entrepreneur, or you, as a marketing director, or you, as a CEO, with the right desire and knowledge, can follow.

Beyond Television

Integrating Radio, Web Advertising, and More

We started in television and for a long time had a predisposition to discuss our marketing strategies in the context of television alone. But in recent years we've branched out into radio, print, and web marketing, finding great value in each. Not just the value one might expect for acquiring more consumers in different channels, but for some distinct advantages each brings to the process of marketing.

Let's start with radio. Some of the first broadcast advertising in America was through radio. It seems every detergent and cigarette manufacturer in the United States had at least one of its own shows on radio. Whether it was the "Palmolive Hour" or the Pall Mall Hour, consumables were branded through dramatic radio shows sponsored by the brand's parent company. Talk show formats sprang up, as well, and this model leaked into the very first years of broadcast television.

Actually, this radio model is still very powerful; we use it frequently to test our own entrepreneurial projects before we go to the effort and expense of shooting a television long form. Here's why:

The radio half hour, or even hour in some markets, is dirt-cheap airtime. You can buy a market for $50 to $100. If you are an entrepreneur and you have an intellectual property, a book, a CD, or even a digestible nutritional supplement, then radio could be your gold rush. The low cost of radio means you need only a few consumer responses to break even and start building your brand in the marketplace. It's true.

If we have an idea that we are unsure of, and want to limit our risk, we can record a radio infomercial on a laptop—literally. Create a talk show with a list of questions that reflect the "sell" of the product. Have the subject of the interview, usually the

191

company founder, "Skype" in and record 30 to 60 minutes of interesting, intelligent discussion. We buy test media for stuff like this all the time, and you would be shocked by how frequently these programs work to profitability, fast. Why?

Radio, beyond being a really inexpensive format, which makes its listenership difficult to trace, sells the time that is not filled to direct response. Guess what? If that time is not being routinely filled, radio stations don't know or care what the audience penetration is at that time. They only worry about broadcast hours for which they are required to produce advertising revenue. If you are the advertising revenue, they simply fill in the spreadsheet and move on.

There's also a creative answer as to why radio is successful. Radio is listening. Listening is picturing. Radio engages the audience deeply. You certainly have heard the story by now of Orson Wells's first radio broadcast of *War of the Worlds* on October 31, 1949. Wells had a good portion of Americans believing that they were in the midst of a Martian invasion.

When you listen to the radio, you do not have the opportunity to look at the host and see if he or she looks like someone you trust. You just have the individual's voice and words. The same is true for the company representative, the call-in testimonials. It all just seems so much easier to believe. Why? Because we like being sold to; we like salespeople, and we love a new, wonderful product. Just make the show about the listener and you have an audience.

The great thing about radio is that because the costs of production and on-air testing are so affordable, you can test many, many creative approaches to perfect your pitch and marketing messages *before* you expand into other areas. Radio is the ideal laboratory for pharmaceuticals, web products, intellectual property, and nutritionals. You can learn everything, even offer from radio, if you are smart, diligent, and patient. Where can you run a true focus group for 50 to 100 bucks? Nowhere!

Radio gives you that ability, along with the prospect of having real consumers respond and pay for the time.

Mind you, radio time is either predominantly late night or weekend, just like television. You are on air when the station does not have its regular scheduled programming. Now here's the caution:

Do not read this book as an inventor and treat the consumer audience as your lab rat. The same rules apply as in all other broadcasts. Your claims must be true and accurate. Your product must have validity and verifiable results. You are considering using the public airwaves to conduct business, so assume the FCC is listening. We are not encouraging scam artists to stick their toes in the water. Plenty have tried, and they get caught. You can lose your home, vehicles, family, and do real jail time for playing fast and loose with any kind of broadcast advertising that is bogus. Lecture over. Be good. It's just as easy—in fact, easier—to find a new, positive, profitable product that you can build a brand around than to take any shortcuts.

If you are just starting out and want to try to build your own brand, learn to use radio wisely, to test new ideas, new products, and develop the proper pitches and offers.

Brand managers and corporate marketers, there is a place for you in radio, as well. Short-form direct response radio does exist, complete with the benefits of a large targeted audience and low, efficient rates. The creative requirements that make radio successful are a clear directed action that you want the consumer to take. Perhaps that is a phone call, a web coupon download, or a visit to your site to register for more information. Be clear on *one specific action*. Don't muddy the water with choices. Too many choices make them commit not to commit.

The web site or the phone number you use in radio is not station-specific, as it is in television. You will sort out your media by caller or visitor zip code later. More repetition is needed to get a radio response because, frankly, you are expecting them to memorize your number or web site. Jingles work great for this. Jingles with a phone number are a sort of mnemonic device that allows the listener to store and access your number like a song. Empire Glass, Inc., is a national affiliation of glass repairmen who belong to an "ad group." They rely on their TV and radio jingle to help drill their number into your head as you meander down the highway. It is an extremely effective technique. Steal it.

Now the question usually comes up: "Isn't all radio advertising DR"? Nope. There are still Coke and Pepsi, auto dealerships, restaurant chains, and hair-cutting salons; but more and more direct response is taking over just due to the nature of products that work on radio. A more accurate statement would be that advertisers that work in the radio space are often smaller companies that really require response-type advertising to help them measure where they can afford to spend very limited marketing budgets. That is exactly where we started in this business, 25 years ago now. Be it radio, television, web, or print, this accountable form of advertising where the effect of every dollar can be measured is just simply a smarter way to do business.

It's often amusing to us that we do business with large multimillion-dollar companies that are completely driven by metrics. They start on the inquiry into direct response and within a week are asking for what they believe are metrics in reach, penetration, and audience size. Those are not actually metrics. Think about it. They are statistics, and not very accurate ones at that. Reach, audience size, and penetration are not particularly useful if you are not selling a darn thing.

Put a $50 advertisement on the radio that drives a consumer to purchase your product for $9.95 by calling a number, now. Sell 10 units. That is a metric. That's measurable, repeatable, and a watermark you can use to judge the success of your marketing. Basing your advertising dollar value on the estimated size of, say, the San Francisco Bay area market, and how many listeners might be tuned into KBAY at 10 o'clock on a Saturday is about as accurate as measuring your sales with a Ouija board. On the other hand, if you put that same ad on and you pay $50 and sell only $50 in goods, then you have the informed power to go back to the station and tell them you would like to continue as an advertiser but that you have discovered that ad placement is worth only $25 to your brand. That's metrics; that's controlling your media spend, and that puts you in the driver's seat.

That budgetary control model is, incidentally, appropriate for television and web, as well. Can you see how DR gives you your power back as an advertiser? You can manipulate the media seller into a weaker position with actual metrics, not the fluff metrics of reach, penetration, and viewership. Now you can afford frequency!

So let's assume you've got your creative ideas clicking on radio. You know your message, or at least you think you do; at the same time, you hopefully have been aggressively dabbling in the marketplace with web DR. Did you even know there was a direct response model working on the web? There is, and here's how we do it.

Online Marketing Is Direct Response

There are several emerging companies serving the web space of direct response, driving sales with both search engine optimization (SEO) and search engine marketing (SEM).

SEO and SEM are the drivers of all web consumer advertising, both nonpaid in the world of SEO, and paid in the world of SEM. SEM is the more familiar of the two, to most companies. The pay-per-click model is primarily driven by the purchase of keywords around your product that force it to appear on the right side of the page in a paid placement during an organic Google search for competitors or those keywords you bought. If the consumer clicks on your ad, you pay more. This is why Google is rich, and you are not.

In direct response, there are web advertising agencies, including ours, that create an entirely self-funded program of web marketing that sells your product. Basically, here's how it works:

You turn control of your entire web marketing venture over to a trusted vendor that uses a "black-box" strategy to integrate paid and nonpaid organic tools to build sales. This works completely independently as a business model to television and radio media. It creates an online direct response campaign that appears everywhere on the web your customer does.

The agency constructs a landing page around a specific direct response offer. This is a transactional site that looks and feels like a very real extension of your company, complete with identical fonts, messaging, and branding. Often, this site is linked to your corporate site, and vice versa. It gives the seamless appearance of being *you*!

The value of this site is what it represents in the present and for the future of the marketing of your company. It is the data-collect site and repository for all you need to know about your customer. All of that learning and data belong to you, forever. Through your own online direct response site, you are then able to test offers in real time, change creative messages, and find out, incrementally, everything you could possibly want to know about every customer silo you have.

What does this cost? Just like the rest of direct response, it's self-funded. The agency is paid a fractional amount of your sale; it is negotiable, but tends to land around 30 percent of the order size. Before you gasp, think. Most manufacturers operating in the traditional model in retail are collecting only a fractional share of the retail goods. Often, only 30 to 50 percent of the cash register ring ends up in the manufacturer's hand. In the online model, you are collecting 70 percent of the retail ring, and you don't have to manage an entire sales channel that, again, is driving the rest of your business.

Are you starting to see how this all integrates with the most powerful marketing model possible?

These links we are building between audience segmentation, consumer silos, messaging, and media, when lumped together, create a new marketing landscape that makes the most efficient use of every marketing dollar you spend.

This model is not futuristic. It is here, now, and yours for the taking. If you are an around-the-kitchen-table entrepreneur, with a lot of energy and smarts, you can do this yourself by enlisting the help of people who make their living entirely on commission. If you are a corporation, you can simply accelerate the brand process, like Han Solo hitting hyperspeed, with very modest resources, compared to conventional marketing.

My father used to say, "You can train a monkey to push a button and get the peanut." He was right; and as mildly insulting as that might sound, we are no different than you. We just found the button first, and are now sharing it!

No matter how small you think you are, or how big you know you are, this model works, over and over. For the first time in history, David can look like Goliath from day one. You have the power and the resources to use this integrated form of television, web, radio, print, and now mobile device, to market like never before. You will be able to find the exact individual you want to find. You will be able to say exactly the right things in the right order and, most importantly, in exactly the right way to get a consumer's individual attention. You will build a sales argument that has the highest probability of success at the maximum price the consumer is willing to pay.

Think about that. If you represent a brand and are willing to take a portion of your business and test, understanding that you can sell more at the same price without the cumbersome mechanics of retailers' supply chain economics, while still driving the retail model, why wouldn't you? That is the reason our industry is exploding into the mainstream brand world. The same reason we were here 25 years ago. Economics necessitated it. The proof was that it pays off. It is truly science, not guesswork; and the more technology advances, the more accurate it becomes.

If we were to vastly oversimplify the interconnection between these moving parts and pieces, we'd tell you the following: Radio defines creative. Web defines offer and audience segmentation. Television drives brand identity and precise consumer vertical sales. Mobile drives direct impulse purchasing. All together, they create brand width and bandwidth. Used properly, this is the most integrated and precise form of self-funded, targeted marketing that has ever been seen. It is the ultimate disguise for the small marketer wanting to look big. It is the ultimate sales channel for the big marketer wanting to increase incremental revenue.

The Backend of Direct Response

Telemarketing, fulfillment, shipping, and credit card processing are what we refer to as the "backend" of the campaign. If you've done this business, you know that refers to everything that happens after the phone rings or someone clicks on the web site. If it is your first time in the business, you will call it the backend because it quickly will become a pain in your backend if you try to manage it yourself. Here's an important note for the corporate marketing expert reading this: Your first thought might be, "Well, we have a catalogue business; we have a shipping department. We can process credit cards; we do so through our existing customer service desk. . . . We even have people who can answer the phone. That way we'll be able to control those expenses and. . . ." *Stop!* Stop right there. You would no sooner hire your spouse and your friends to answer calls and pick and pack orders in your garage than you would get into this business. You do not have the specialized resources internally that it takes to pull off this business profitably.

There is an entire industry full of experts who, for 30 years, have been working out every single kink and headache in the backend business. It is a tiger that will eat you if you even attempt it by yourself. Do not consider it for a second. Too gentle for you? Your boss may read this book, and we're telling him or her right now that only a bonehead would try to pull this off. You will waste precious time and money learning what we are giving you here for free—the facts!

Most corporations that have attempted this—even mail-order companies—have abandoned doing it themselves and hired professionals that do this 24/7. So should you.

The Phone Rings: Who Answers It?

There is an entire science behind call conversion. The phone script is as important as the marketing plan; even we don't write these. We make some suggestions and let the experts handle it from there. Often, the call center experts come back with suggestions for offers and pricing structures after they have spoken to live customers with money in hand. Often, they optimize sales better than what we've previously tested. Remember, assume you know nothing! It does not matter where the better idea comes from; we just want to implement it as soon as possible.

Telemarketing agencies are also renowned for teaching you how to turn your customer complaint and warranty issue lines into profit centers. It's true. If you build your business model right, and treat your complaining customer right, you have the chance to gain a consumer for life and build reputation. We once worked with a company that sold small appliances—primarily, countertop cooking products. When a customer would call in, for whatever reason, the agency rep would instantly take care of the complaint, no matter what. If the device required replacement, out went a replacement, along with a free gift in the package, as a thank-you for alerting the company to a potential failure issue. Often, that gift was a very nice, branded knife. A week later, a rep from the agency would call the consumer to make sure he or she got the replacement, and the consumer would be up-sold to either a complete set of knives at 50 percent off or a second device at 50 percent off, as a gift for a friend. The customer service department actually turned a profit the first six months after implementing the strategy, and any Better Business Bureau issues evaporated.

There are between 40 and 50 telemarketing agencies in the United States, and a few abroad, that are devoted to direct response marketing. They are very capable. The process of selecting the one that is right for you should take into consideration a number of factors, including the type of good or service you are selling, the offer, the price, and the consumer demographic.

There are telemarketers that specialize by category. That is, the predominance of their clientele are, for example, in the exercise or fitness equipment business, weight-loss intellectual property, DVDs, and the like. There are also soft goods specialists, web goods specialists, cooking device specialists. The list of categories goes on.

There are also companies that specialize by offer value. Lead-generation companies and soft-offer sales comprise their own category. Anyone who has ever been invited to an investment seminar or time-share presentation understands that process. It's appropriate for some legitimate and successful products to take a two-step close process. Some home furniture wholesale clubs, construction and real estate products, even automobiles, are successfully sold and monetized through direct response lead-generation campaigns. There are telesales companies that specialize in receiving these calls and prequalifying leads according to your strata.

Fulfillment: Getting Your Customers Their Products

Fulfillment is similar to telemarketing. A fulfillment company is one that receives the digital order from the call center as it comes in and physically packs and ships your product. For all intents and purposes, it is your warehouse and distribution center for the direct response business. There are numerous fulfillment companies in the United States, and you will decide which one will pick and pack your orders, based on a number of factors.

The first is location. Are you manufacturing goods in Asia, with your port of call in Los Angeles? Perhaps you have a larger product and so rely on the Port of Louisiana and the rail system. Are the bulk of your consumers in the Sunbelt, driving an advantage to distribute from the South Central United States? These are all considerations.

The second is shipment expertise. There are some companies that specialize in home appliance and large exercise equipment. Others are expert in intellectual property and small electrics. There are others that focus entirely on foods, dried foods, and nutritional supplements.

The key is to measure the fulfillment company's expertise with like items, as the more efficient it is at picking and packing items like yours, the more success you will have. Larger companies may have greater purchasing power when it comes to postage rates, and get you a better price. Smaller companies may find your start-up account is more important to the growth of their business overall and will provide you better attention and customer service.

Both the telemarketing and fulfillment businesses seem to fall into a similar cycle as other American companies. Successful senior employees of existing larger companies typically start new companies in these fields. These individuals are often frustrated with the inefficiencies that they experience daily. Inefficiency is usually driven by the systemization that running a large organization requires. When these individuals start, they have found a service area of the industry, or even a client, they can "steal" from their previous companies and that they can service very well. They are hungry for business, which drives their personal attention to your account and company. This stimulates growth and momentum, and they eventually become big enough to be acquired by one of the larger players; or they get too big for their britches and their one golden goose flies away and they are left with a very serious problem of real estate and/or human resources overhead. It takes a lot of space to run a warehouse business, and a lot of folks to run a call center. If one or two of their largest clients go away, and they get caught holding a big fat lease and supporting a couple of hundred employees, they're lights out!

Often, you will want to find a call center and fulfillment company that are somewhere in the middle of that cycle. We do that for clients every day.

Credit Card Processing: Getting Paid

Credit card processing agencies also known as a "merchant banking relationship" is really the last step in the selection of players that will help you make your business happen. A credit card processing agency is usually chosen at the same time as fulfillment, because the two components are so closely tied together. You see, after a phone or Internet order is taken, it is digitally passed, along with the consumer's credit card data, to the fulfillment center. After—and only after—the order is packed and shipped, may you pass the credit card data to the card processing agency, to ping the card. Ping the card before you ship the order, go to jail. It's that simple. As a corporation dealing with the FCC and the FTC, and because you are advertising over the airwaves, the process of taking consumers' credit cards is very closely watched. This is the number-one way that bogus television and Internet marketers get in trouble.

Unscrupulous companies will attempt to charge cards before actual inventory exists, to falsely fund their ventures. It is against the law, and many people have done serious time for committing this crime.

As an entrepreneur, you will want to have at least fulfillment levels of inventory to start testing your program—somewhere in the neighborhood of 1,000 units—before you air. As you test your plan and find success, there are plenty of reliable and reputable ways to gain long-term financing, to build both inventory and media purchasing for long-term success. That sort of funding is very common, and there are a variety of companies that exist within the direct response model that fund success.

CHAPTER
16

Conclusion

What do you require? A long-form campaign? A short-form campaign? Both? Let's say you decide. Asking what it costs is a fair question; but if you were to draw a parallel to the construction world, it's a little like asking, "What does it cost to build a house?" We all know the answer to that depends on a lot of factors, including land development, labor costs, materials cost, and the size, quality, and trimmings.

Infomercial production is exactly the same. Assuming you have already come through the "development" stage and you have a saleable product, now you will have to start outlining the creative strategy that best represents your product and invites the market to participate with sincerity.

Brass Tacks: What Does This Cost?

Some full-length infomercials cost $250,000; some cost north of $1 million, after talent considerations. We work on both types. Some infomercials for intellectual property cost far less. Dean Graziosi's real estate show is shot in his vehicle; it has absolutely no production value whatsoever, but it feels real! I would guess he didn't spend more than $15,000 shooting the host segment. Add in graphics, music, and tape trafficking, and he had a hit show for $40 grand; but it looks like it. Graziosi is building a brand around his name, not a quality-constructed product. There will be no expanded product line beyond him. He *is* the brand.

If you have an intellectual property product like Graziosi's, by all means, do it yourself! The passion you bring to the program will far outweigh the lack of production value. For the rest of us who are truly interested in brand building, you can expect to spend between $500,000 and $1 million to get into this business in a strong-branded way.

Inventors: Don't close the book! There are avenues to get this kind of money. If your product holds the true promise of branded success, if it is not a dog dish shaped like a toilet bowl, you have a big opportunity.

If you are not an inventor, if you are a marketing specialist, a salesperson, or a CEO, you will instantly recognize the incredible value of those numbers. Imagine getting into business for well under a million dollars in a marketing vehicle that offers the promise of becoming measurably profitable in real time, fast—get back the cost of production, the cost of product development, and the cost of media in under a year. Year 2, expand into retail; introduce new products and build brand value, to make you look and feel like a new category creator and leader. Repeat the process, and by year 5 you are where most companies are at in about year 15 or 20.

This is the ultimate value of the direct response long form with a USP, and the Direct Demographic Media Messaging of short form. These two powerful methods short-circuit the traditional business mechanics that slowly expand consumer awareness, purchase behavior, brand building, and establish a powerful competitive space in the marketplace. Direct response is *the* tool of the modern entrepreneur or the corporation that thinks entrepreneurially.

Accept the fact that you are most likely not going to create a realistic strategy to be a billionaire in this life. At the same time, the billionaire entrepreneurs didn't set out for that, either. Don't make a million dollars from anybody; make a single dollar from everybody. That's the brand game. That's the winning strategy.

Accept the reality that there is no reason on earth you cannot be a millionaire with at least $10 million in the bank if you come up with the right idea and drive sales through this tried-and-true process. I do not say this to give you false hope or to make you feel good about buying this book. I say it because we've done it; we've seen it, we've lived it, and we replicate it. We've seen people who are not all that brilliant or special duplicate the process. Remember, we didn't start out as marketing PhDs. We are normal people who had an extraordinary marketing experience and learned from it. We are not arrogant know-it-alls, here to say we invented the industry; we didn't. There are plenty of other guys who did it their way, too. We *can* say we were in the right place at the right time, learning the right things to do. Now that you have this book in your hands, so are you.

Welcome to the club. Learn from our good fortune and experience. Make them yours. We have duplicated this process so many times it has become second nature to us, and we know it truly is not that mysterious or difficult. It is about putting your ego aside, assuming you know nothing, and looking at sales from a very simple perspective. Learn to talk to one customer at a time and sell in the most basic, honest way you can, and people will respond. Trust your product.

You will learn even more by experiencing this process just one time than we can ever express in print. Walk through the process and you will get the reward. When you do, you too will be infected by the understanding of the immense power of direct response. You will be the expert. Guaranteed.

Bye now!

INDEX